A CHALLENGE TO CHANGE

Practical experiences
of building user-led services

Edited by
Peter Beresford and Tessa Harding

Published 1993
by the National Institute for Social Work
5 Tavistock Place, London WC1H 9SN
Tel: 071 387 9681
© National Institute for Social Work and the authors

ISBN 0 902789 85 6

British Library Cataloguing in Publication Data
A catalogue record for this book is available from the
British Library

Page design and layout by Diana Birch
Cover design by Pat Kahn
Printed by Repro City, London EC2A 4BH
This publication is also available in audio-cassette
form. Its presentation is in line with the Royal National
Institute for Blind People guidance on the production of
publications for people who are visually impaired.

Dedication

Gareth Walton, one of the contributors to this book,
died earlier this year. He was a member of the
Community Health Team Quality Assurance Group in
Hammersmith and Fulham Council's HIV Service. The
Group was essentially a user-led initiative set up by
people living with HIV/AIDS in partnership with the
team I work in, to come together not only to look at
improving our service delivery but also to put across,
on their terms, what it actually means to live with a
life threatening illness.

Derek, another Group member, wrote "We're the free
souls not bound by bureaucratic rules. We have
ambition and vision". This work is dedicated to both
Gareth and Derek who are no longer with us.

It is also dedicated to other members of the Quality
Assurance Group who still play an active role, and
those Group members who have died. They have taught
the team and myself so much about what it means to
involve people in service delivery, and the effect that
HIV/AIDS has on individuals' lives. For that we will
always be in their debt.

Andy Brown
Community Worker (HIV)
Hammersmith and Fulham Social Services Department

Acknowledgements

We have many people to thank for their help in producing this book. We would particularly like to thank all the people in disabled people's and service users' organisations and their allies upon whose experience and achievements the book rests. We would also like to thank the Joseph Rowntree Foundation, whose financial support made possible both the publication of the book and its availability to service users, and the participation of many disabled people and other service users at the conference upon which it is based. Finally we want to thank Ann Vandersypen, Nahid Ziaee, Margaret Hogan and Daphne Statham of the National Institute for Social Work, Linda Ward and Janet Lewis of the Joseph Rowntree Foundation, Suzy Croft of Open Services Project, Andy Brown and Sarah McClinton of Hammersmith and Fulham Social Services Department and Suki Montford for all their help and support.

The **Joseph Rowntree Foundation** has supported this project as part of its programme of research and innovative development projects, which it hopes will be of value to policy makers and practitioners. The facts presented and views expressed in this report, however, are those of the authors and not necessarily those of the Foundation.

NATIONAL INSTITUTE
FOR SOCIAL WORK

OPEN
SERVICES
PROJECT

JR
JOSEPH
ROWNTREE
FOUNDATION

CommunityCare
The independent voice of social work

CONTENTS

Foreword

TERRY PHILPOT

For service users, the last few years have been the best of times, and in some ways, the worst of times.

The best - because official sanction was given to their central importance in community care when the Social Services Inspectorate said of the National Health Service and Community Care Act "The rationale for this reorganisation is the empowerment of users and carers" (Social Services Inspectorate, 1991). While this may only be a marker on the long road journeyed by service users, rather than the final destination, it is a significant one. We have come a long way down that road since the Barclay Committee on the roles and tasks of social workers came into being in 1980 without a service user member. Six years later the Wagner Committee on residential care made the same mistake. But the subsequent Wagner Development Group learned from it: the third Wagner Report, *Positive Answers*, was very strongly influenced by service users (Wagner Development Group, 1993). By 1993 criticism of the exclusion of service users from the Department of Health Community Care Support Force was not only remedied towards the end of its life, but when it was wound up it was succeeded by a Users and Carers Group to monitor the reforms for the next three years.

The worst - because the Social Services Inspectorate's words and other positive initiatives had long shadows cast across them. Among these was the shadow of the

guidance from the same Inspectorate which seemed
to move local authorities away from user-led
assessment, by advising that service users' unmet
need was not to be recorded. Another shadow, which
Kathryn Ellis's research into assessment showed, was
assessors bringing to assessment value judgements
about whether service users were "deserving" or
"undeserving". They were often ill-equipped also, to
offer much more than a narrow range of specialist
and segregated provision (Ellis, 1993). And then there
has been the government's announcement that it
would not implement sections 1-3 of the 1986
Disabled Persons (Services, Consultation and
Representation) Act, which would have allowed a
right of independent representation and information.

But despite these setbacks one thing is certain -
service users have asserted themselves. They have
made it known that they are, like Eliot's Magi, "no
longer at ease here, in the old dispensation", where
they were expected to take what was offered.
Concepts of citizenship and rights have replaced old
ideas of benevolence and good intentions.

This book is emblematic of the new dispensation, the
new direction being forged by service users and their
allies. It is based on contributions given at a
conference in advance of the full implementation of
the National Health Service and Community Care
Act. When we advertised the conference, we referred
to the danger that service users' interests might be
overlooked in the scramble for reform. Fortunately,
despite the setbacks, that has not proved to be the
case.

Both Jenny Morris and Peter Beresford refer in their

contributions to the need for allies. The latter reminds us of the important fact that workers too can be disabled. But notwithstanding structural difficulties and organisational obstacles that militate against user involvement, it is still not uncommon to hear workers being dismissive of the roles that service users can play. Olive Stevenson and Phyllida Parsloe have made the same point with their contention that service users cannot be empowered unless staff are empowered, and that empowerment is not a technical change - something that is put in place in one part of the organisation - but that the whole culture must be an empowering one (Parsloe and Stevenson, 1993).

There is another important, yet frequently overlooked point about user involvement: it is not cheap, either in terms of money or time. We recognised this in the planning of the conference. The large number of service users present, which accounted for at least a third of those attending, was due to the generosity of the Joseph Rowntree Foundation making bursaries available for service user participants. Linda Ward, the Foundation's Disability Programme Adviser, joined the editors of this book and me on the planning team. If service users are to be real partners they need the wherewithal to be so. They need to be paid for their contribution and their expenses need to be met, and to be met speedily without undue form-filling and bureaucracy. They may well need other kinds of support too: secretarial, the use of office equipment and office space. They may need training in how meetings are run, support when they attend them and briefings beforehand. Professional staff take all this for granted. Service users should be able to also. Yet it seems all too easy for professionals to overlook such matters, just when the professional mould is being broken by the introduction of the hitherto unheard voices and the physical presence of those who use services.

Change can be painful. It is disrupting. *A Challenge to Change* is the title of this book, as it was of the conference. This book shows, in a very practical way, how that challenge is being met.

Introduction

PETER BERESFORD AND TESSA HARDING

This book brings together contributors with many different backgrounds: disabled people and other service users, practitioners, managers, trainers, advisers, researchers, consultants and academics. They reflect a wide variety of perspectives, cultures, values and approaches. Some of the contributions are very personal; others are more concerned with organisations and structures. Some are short, others longer. One of the particular strengths of this collection is its enormous diversity. But what unites it is the practical experience people bring to building user-led services. There is no one route to user-led services and the contributors offer a wide range of insights into how they can be built.

This diversity is also reflected in the style of contributions. Many different voices are to be heard here. We have deliberately sought not to impose a standardised format or style. Some contributors were used to writing, others were not. They were offered any support they needed. In one case this meant having a discussion, transcribing it and agreeing an edited version, so that the contributor could say exactly what they wanted. Contributions were edited with contributors retaining final editorial control.

We received a wide range of comments, both written and spoken, about the conference upon which this book is based. Participants identified positive features and some problems. They found it "exciting and challenging", "useful to be able to share our experiences with others with similar problems", and valued the fact that service users led many of the sessions. But they would also have liked more opportunities for participants to contribute, to speak for and about themselves; for there to be smaller groups, "more open structures, and creative language for non-readers and people who use other languages".

Language is a central issue in building user-led services. It's an important issue for this book too and although we have tried to make the book as accessible as possible, we recognise that it will still not be accessible to everyone.

Language is also contentious in this field, because it is often used to disempower and oppress people. In their contribution, Jackie Downer and Peter Ferns refer specifically to the issue of terminology. While there is no agreed language - language changes over time and most terms carry some negative associations for somebody - we have tried to use terms which will cause the least offence to people.

To help readers negotiate the variety of material in the book, we have organised it in five parts. The opening discussion sets the scene, exploring some of the issues and problems currently facing people working to build user-led services. Part Two focuses on initiatives by service users to increase their involvement in and control of the services they use and the lives they lead. This leads on to the examples presented in Part Three of participatory projects initiated by service providers. Part Four explores some models for involving people which have wider application and may be used in other contexts. The final Part of the book brings together the experiences and ideas of service users, ending with a vision for the future.

The main sections of the book are punctuated by shorter contributions which look at what working together can mean as well as some of the problems and opportunities that people now face. We hope that *A Challenge to Change* offers readers something of the sense of discovery and excitement that building user-led services and user-controlled alternatives promises.

Part One:

Setting the Agenda

A Programme for Change: Current Issues in User Involvement and Empowerment

PETER BERESFORD

TAKING STOCK AND GETTING THINGS CLEAR

Now is a helpful time to take stock of community care and user involvement. Not only is community care policy at a watershed, but the terms of the debate are now being transformed by disabled people and other recipients of services. Much has happened in a relatively short time (Croft and Beresford, 1979). While welfare service users have long had their own discussions and discourse about the exclusion and oppression they experience, this has largely been hidden, ignored and unreported. It is only in the last ten to 15 years that they have been able to force their views on to public, political and social policy agendas. This has also been linked with wider political, economic and social change.

The current conventional wisdom in community care and social policy more broadly is that service users' involvement is essential. A rhetorical commitment has been made to it. Politicians, policy makers, managers, researchers and professionals have shown their capacity to learn the language of involvement and empowerment. But being flavour of the month is not necessarily beneficial to any cause's health.

The issues around user involvement and empowerment aren't straightforward. They are complex, subtle and sometimes ambiguous. Because of this it's important to try and get things *clearer*. It's a big task for all of us, whether we are concerned as service providers, service users or both, but it's a particular priority for those of us on the receiving end of services. Only then can we begin to work out how best we can use the limited resources we have and what we should be pressing politicians, agencies, services and funders to be doing to help people get what they want in their lives.

OPENING AND CLOSING

This is a time of enormous change, conflicts and contradictions in public policy. I want to look at a number of *tensions* in what's happening in community care, where some developments seem to be pulling in one direction, but others are also pulling in another. The first of these tensions is where some things seem to be *opening* and creating opportunities, others to be *closing* and cutting us off from them. Let's look at these two, beginning with the things which are opening.

Opening

- Whatever their limitations, the National Health Service and Community Care Act and the Children Act both make provisions which provide a legislative requirement for people's involvement. They offer people chances to comment and complain, to have a voice in what happens to them and to be involved in planning.

- During the 1980s and early 1990s there has been a massive growth in the number, strength and significance of organisations of people who use community care services. It is becoming increasingly difficult for government and service providers to ignore these local, regional and national organisations of people with physical and sensory impairments, people with learning difficulties, survivors of the mental health system, people affected by HIV and older people. They provide service users with their own distinct collective voices as well as support, self-help and opportunities to speak for themselves.

• The critiques of disabled people's and other service user organisations give new meanings to ideas and analyses which were previously the property of service providers and professionals. The social model of disability emphasises the oppression and discrimination people face from society because of their impairments or distress. Independence is reconceived to mean ensuring people the support to enable them to live independently, instead of expecting them to live without support. The idea of "independent living" has been developed as a preferred alternative to "community care", emphasising people's rights and capacities instead of their dependence and incapacity.

• An increasing number of professionals, including social workers, nurses and psychologists, want to work with service users in more equal and responsive ways. Some of them support service users as allies, working alongside them, without taking over and offering access to agency resources, information and expertise.

- The development by disabled people and other community care service users of services under their own control. These include both self-controlled individual services, like personal assistance schemes, and collective services controlled by service users. Such user-led services offer pioneering models and prototypes for more general implementation by statutory services.

- One spin-off of the government's interest in the market and purchase of service in public provision is that it highlights that people have as much right to decent services from community care as they have when they buy something on the high street. The introduction of ideas of consumerism into welfare policy and provision may have disadvantages, but it has also encouraged a changing climate which emphasises people's rights as consumers and helps to raise their expectations.

- This is the age of the citizen as well as of the public service consumer. Citizens charters from central government, political parties and local authorities for specific services as well as in relation to government more generally all highlight our rights and entitlements as citizens and service users and encourage people to recognise their rights to a say, redress and quality in relation to the state.

Closing
- The prevailing pattern is of restrictions and cuts in expenditure and resources both for dedicated community care services and other public provision. Most local authorities are making cuts

in social services. Their organisations argue that insufficient money has been made available by government for community care.

- Community care services which people value are being reduced, stopped or changed without their agreement. These include home help and other domiciliary support, legal and advice services, occupational therapy, physiotherapy and district nurse services. The role and tasks of home helps, for example, are undergoing fundamental change, without effective consultation with either service workers or service users.

- The Independent Living Fund has been closed, payments to disabled people for support are being capped and there are growing fears among disabled people of being re-institutionalised.

- Charges are increasingly being made for services and charges are also being raised, effectively restricting and rationing access to services.

- During the 1980s, changed financial arrangements and the government's commitment to the commercial sector resulted in an increase in the number of older people and people with learning difficulties housed in institutional accommodation. So far there has been no sign that this is being reversed with the full implementation of community care legislation.

CASH AND CULTURE: PRE-REQUISITES FOR INVOLVEMENT AND EMPOWERMENT

What can really be done if there aren't adequate resources? All the indications are that if it is to be effective and anti-discriminatory, user-involvement requires resources (Beresford and Croft, 1993). Having said that, we should also remember that even without more money there can be change in cultures and attitudes. And more money could just mean more of the same.

The 1992 report *Great Expectations...and Spending on Social Services* by the Policy Forum evidenced what people who use services know only too well. There is not enough money. It's unequally distributed and what you get depends on where you happen to live (Harding, 1992). At the same time, there's more to it than just money. It's what it is spent on, where it goes, who decides, who controls the money, who gets the money, that matter too.

The Policy Forum is a group of organisations which includes the British Association of Social Workers, Association of Directors of Social Services, Social Care Association, National Institute for Social Work, National Council for Voluntary Organisations and the Joseph Rowntree Foundation. But there are no disabled people's organisations among them; no organisations of users of services. You might ask why the British Council of Organisations of Disabled People, the United Kingdom Advocacy Network, Survivors Speak Out, People First and organisations of older people, people affected by HIV and other groups aren't among them. Is there a place any longer for forums where this isn't the case? Surely it is time that user-led organisations like these participate in forums like this on equal terms.

Otherwise where is the money going to go, if ever it becomes available: to service providers and their highly paid consultants or to user-led initiatives and service users and their organisations? Will it really make possible change for the better? Happily, in this particular case there has been progress since the publication of the report. After comment from service users, the Policy Forum set up an initiative to look at "the shape of user-led services", with a working group which includes both service users and service providers.

Both culture change and cash resources seem to be needed if involvement and empowerment are to flourish. In the absence of a culture consistent with people's involvement, resources are more likely to disempower than empower. Lack of cash stifles and undermines cultural change.

Different Approaches to Involvement

Getting things clearer will help us concentrate our effort most effectively, work out what we want to do and where we want to go. I have discussed different approaches to involvement elsewhere in more detail (Croft and Beresford, 1992). But I think it's important to touch on it here, because it leads us to much broader issues around people's involvement and empowerment. It's certainly another issue that needs to be clarified. It also highlights another of the tensions in community care and user-involvement.

People are not agreed about what they mean by involvement. There seem to be two main overlapping but different models in people's minds. The first of these is concerned with *comment*. It seems to be an extension of the public participation programmes and provisions of the 1960s and 1970s. On to this has been grafted the government's interest from the

1980s in consumerism. It is probably most helpful to think of it as a kind of "supermarket" or consumerist model of involvement. If service providers ask people what they want, the argument goes, then they'll get more efficient, more effective, more economic services. They'll be better managed and more responsive.

The second approach to involvement is concerned with *control* . This can perhaps best be understood as the empowerment or democratic approach. While it has its own distinct history, it has some similarities with grassroots initiatives for involvement and empowerment in the 1960s and 1970s, which were linked to campaigning and community development, particularly among disadvantaged and oppressed groups. Here people want to have more control over their own lives. They want more say. They want to be in charge of what happens to them. They want to be treated like anybody else.

Both of these models of, or approaches to, involvement are of value. Both have contributions to make. They have overlaps. For example, in one way or another, both are concerned with change. But don't confuse them. They aren't the same.

The consumerist approach is service-centred and seems primarily concerned with meeting the needs of services. The democratic approach is people-centred and is concerned with meeting people's rights and needs. The first one has come from service providers - from policy makers, agencies and experts; the second one from service users, their organisations and allies.

When I meet people who are recipients of or eligible for community care services, they say things like "I want a real job"; "I need more money"; "I want a home of my own"; "I want to be able to go out and get to the shops like anyone else"; "the two of us want to live together".

I can understand this. It fits with my experience and aspirations. But I don't hear many service users saying "I'm really anxious that social services can get their restructuring of day care services in place"; or "a new data collection system at social services headquarters could really work marvels".

People want more say in their *lives*, not just in services. Services aren't their primary concern. They don't see themselves solely in terms of services, but much beyond them. This is one reason why some people don't like the terms user and user involvement. They don't see themselves as service users. They may see themselves as disabled, as survivors or as people first. But not just service users.

However, in my experience, when you use community care or other welfare services, you can find yourself ending up using a widening range of services. It's like a pebble dropped in a pool, with you in the middle of ever-increasing circles of services. For me this has meant income support, mental health services, social services, environmental health, appeals tribunal, housing benefits, housing advice, unemployment service. For other people there may be different kinds and patterns of services involved. There's something important to say about such services:

- many of them are unpleasant
- many of them are frightening
- many of them are humiliating
- often they make you feel really bad.

17

Your life becomes centred on services. But that doesn't mean you want it to be. This reflects and leads me to another series of tensions in community care. These are:

- between being included and kept out
- between services and citizens
- between welfare and our civil rights
- between a focus on services and a focus on the wider world.

INVOLVEMENT IN THE MAINSTREAM

Involvement is not just about people being involved in community care services, but participating in and having a say in mainstream life. As Mike Oliver, the disability writer and activist, says:

> "Disability is a human rights issue requiring political action rather than a social problem requiring welfare provision" (Oliver, 1991/2).

People don't want to live in a separate state of welfare. They don't want votes in a homeland, but not in their own country. Even South Africa is starting to move beyond that. So must community care and social policy here. The issue of involvement and user involvement must no longer be treated in isolation like this, restricted to separate, segregated social services.

The issue of participation is then reduced from people's right to participate fully in society and have a say in it, to being involved in the running of welfare services they might prefer not to receive. These are quite different meanings of involvement.

Having a say in separate welfare services doesn't make up for being restricted to them. Bill Jordan, the social work writer and commentator, made this clear nearly 20 years ago. He rejected social work which provided special services to "welfare cases", denying people access to the mainstream, and condemned social services for perpetuating protective but infantilising provision for a sector of the population. He argued:

> "People's citizenship is reduced, not increased by the giving of second-hand goods and second-hand sympathy" (Jordan, 1975).

What participation and involvement must mean - what empowerment means - is being able to participate fully in society. We can see that reflected in three key objectives of the disabled people's movement. These are for:

- *access to the mainstream* : to jobs, housing, education, recreation, the environment, public transport, to vote, and so on;

- *a say in support services* : the services we need to ensure our independence and inclusion, to ensure that they are the right ones;

- *securing our civil rights* : to be equal citizens alongside other people.

The current strategies of the disabled people's movement also broadly match these goals. They are for:

- *anti-discrimination legislation* : to challenge oppression and safeguard their rights;

- *freedom of information act* : so people know what's happening to them;

- *support for their organisations* : so they can effectively organise, involve disabled people broadly and work together for change and involvement in and beyond the service world.

These are also important goals for other movements. People want *support* and people want their *rights*. But when we say what we want, we run into another of these problems or tensions.

BEING REPRESENTATIVE

This is the tension between speaking for ourselves and being "representative". Traditionally when other people spoke for disabled people, older people and the other welfare service users, it wasn't questioned. Now when people are themselves challenging this, when they say that they want to speak for themselves, instead of having someone else talking on their behalf, they are accused of being unrepresentative. They are told "they aren't typical"; "who are they to talk?"; "they're just the articulate ones"!

Service providers identify this as a key problem. Now there are real difficulties for rights, users and other self-help organisations to involve people as widely as they want, when they haven't got the resources or workers to do it. But the argument about representativeness is also a convenient one to keep people out. However the buck really stops with service providers. If they feel people who get involved aren't representative, then the responsibility lies with them to change this. As things are they often make it so that only the most determined, the most confident, the most experienced people have a chance to get involved. It's so *difficult* to be involved. There are two key components that are needed if that's to change and it is to become possible for more people to be able to get involved. These are *access* and *support* . Both are crucial. If there's no way in to make change, then you can only bang your head against a brick wall. If there's no support, only the few will be able to use any chances there are.

Access means being able to get into the political process, having a vote and being able to vote, to become a councillor, to become an MP, to be able to learn how the system works. It means services and organisations which are physically accessible, so you can get into them and you feel comfortable in them. It means services which match everyone's needs, men and women, black and white, old or young, whatever people's sexual orientation. Access means opportunities to make change, on sub-committees, working groups, planning groups, in the political and administrative structures of organisations and services. It means opportunities which are there all the time, not just here today and gone tomorrow, like some quick consultation exercise. Then we can get involved, learn the skills and get better at it.

Support is just as important. We don't live in a society where getting involved is usual for most people. The lesson most of us are taught at school and afterwards is to do what we're told. Welfare services have tended to make this worse for people who use them by restricting people's confidence, skills and self-esteem.

People may not know what's possible, may not like to ask for too much, are frightened of being told off, don't like to complain or don't know how to. Support means support in:

- *personal development* : to increase people's expectations, assertiveness, self-confidence and self-esteem;

- *skill development* : to build the skills they need to participate and to develop their own alternative approaches to involvement;

- *practical support* : to be able to take part, including information, child care, transport, meeting places, advocacy;

- *support for equal opportunities* : provision for people with physical and sensory impairments, deaf people, people without verbal communication, non-readers, people for whom English is not their first language and people with intellectual impairments to get involved on equal terms;

- *support for people to get together and work in groups*: including administrative expenses, payment for workers, training and development costs.

Support also means specific initiatives to enable the involvement of black people and members of other minority ethnic communities, otherwise all the evidence suggests they'll continue to be excluded and marginalised. This means additional resources and efforts to involve them in any schemes for user-involvement set up by services and additional resources for disabled people's and other organisations to make sure that the anti-racist attitudes and approaches they work for are matched by the necessary cash for development workers and other resources needed to engage all communities equally.

TENSIONS BETWEEN SERVICE USERS AND PROVIDERS

There are two last tensions I want to discuss. The first of these is the tensions between service providers and service users. The two have different aims and interests. Often they are in conflict. It's important to recognise this. But I want to draw a distinction between service users, service agencies like social services, and their *workers*. Sometimes it can seem as if it is a case of both service users and workers versus agencies - agencies which are frequently depersonalising, hierarchical and disempowering.

It's helpful here to recognise the overlaps that exist between service workers and users - the many things we have in common. Remember that at the sharp end, many people in both groups are women, many are black, many are on low income, and most may feel powerless. This is in sharp contrast with large agencies and their highly paid "hands-off" managers, consultants and policy makers.

One thing that I have learned from teaching social workers is the understanding that can grow from shared oppressions and the things which we have in common. I've learned this particularly from the black students I teach. Sometimes the process of becoming a human service worker almost seems like one designed to make us forget or reject our common humanity and our similarities, as well as acknowledging our differences. Workers may have mental distress. Workers may be disabled.

It's important to recognise, build on and encourage
these overlaps. We need to support the increased
recruitment of disabled people, people affected by
HIV, people with mental distress and others who
want to work to support people's independent living,
as part of broader equal opportunities employment
policies. We need to ensure there is support for such
workers in agencies instead of them facing
discrimination, and a lack of support and sensitivity,
and having to deny who they are.

Service users and progressive workers need to
strengthen the links and alliances that already exist
between them. Workers can also learn a lot from
service users and their organisations about the
personal support they get from each other. And
workers need to be involved in any efforts to involve
service users. It's no use for politicians or managers to
try and dump user involvement on them. They won't
own it. It won't work. Instead they have got to be
properly involved in the process. Their ideas and
experience are important. Service users'
empowerment won't come through the additional
disempowerment of face to face workers.

INVOLVEMENT AND TOKENISM

The last tension I want to touch on is that between
involvement which offers people more say and
control, and tokenism. People want to get involved to
influence what happens, to change things; to have
more say in their lives. But that isn't always why
people are asked to get involved and it's not the only
purpose it serves. People's participation is also used
for:

- *Delay* or to stop things happening. Action is made to wait on people's involvement. The need to consult, to set up "self-advocacy" groups, is used as a reason for doing nothing.

- *Incorporation and co-option* to suck people in and keep them quiet. People are drawn into participatory arrangements which limit and divert their effective action.

- *Legitimation* to make things look right. People's ineffectual involvement is used to give the appearance of their agreement and consent to pre-determined decisions and plans. Participation serves as a public relations and window-dressing exercise. It's used to obtain the minority involvement of members of oppressed groups, unrelated to the representative structures established by their organisations.

AUDITING INVOLVEMENT

Because of these problems, it's crucial we develop ways to *audit involvement* , to find out what it's really offering and what it achieves. Otherwise how do we know what we're letting ourselves in for and whether it's worthwhile getting involved? The bottom line for user involvement is:

- where is the cash spent on it going?
- who is being involved?
- what redistribution of power if any is there?
- what changes is it leading to in people's lives?
- how is it helping people secure and safeguard their rights?

INVOLVEMENT AND EQUALITIES

That leads me finally to the importance of seven *equalities* we should be aiming for. These are:

Equality of credibility

What service users say warrants equal weight with what service providers say. As things are, too often it's not what you say but who says it. There's a hierarchy of credibility as well as of access. What service users and their organisations say is put at the bottom of the heap. But it can no longer be dismissed as partial, anecdotal or unimportant, any more than the evidence, proposals and testimony of women and black people can. More weight must be given to what people who use services say. More opportunities should be provided for people to express their viewpoints on their own terms.

Equal access to resources

There must be a level playing field over where resources for user involvement go. This issue should be high on the agenda of both funders and service providers. Something strange is happening if while the talk is about user involvement, most of the resources for it are still going to traditional service providers, professionals and researchers - to organisations *for* rather than organisations *of* disabled people and other service users. Yet all the signs are that this is how most of the resources for research and development on user involvement are still distributed. The situation needs to be closely monitored.

Equalisation of power

Both of the previous issues are part of a broader one - the redistribution of power between service users and service providers. Power still lies predominantly with services and service providers. It remains to be seen how this will be affected by the new arrangements for community care. User involvement raises issues of power and empowerment. These are often ducked or underplayed. Instead they should be properly acknowledged. People's involvement and empowerment are ultimately about the redistribution of power.

Equality between black and white people, women and men

In the past participatory schemes have often mirrored rather than challenged the oppressions of our society - pushing out groups facing discrimination, confirming and sometimes even legitimating their exclusion rather than doing something about it. All schemes for involvement and empowerment must take account of this issue and develop written-in strategies for tackling it. User involvement should be an expression of equal opportunities policy, not the opposite of it.

Equal access to employment

I've already referred to this. People who use community care services should have equal access to employment in community care services as part of broader equal opportunities employment policy. Their expertise in their own experience provides them with a crucial starting point for supporting others.

Equality between different groups

People included in many different groups receive or are eligible for community care services. These include children and older people, homeless people, people with learning difficulties, people affected by

HIV, people with chronic or terminal illness, people with physical and sensory impairments, people with alcohol and drug related problems. They face different issues and problems. They face different kinds of stigma and discrimination. Some are disposed of by the criminal justice system as well as by support services. They have achieved different degrees of success in their struggles for greater say and control in their lives. The rights and needs of all these groups must be recognised and secured. The efforts of politicians and service providers to play them off against each other, to do something for one at the expense of another, must be resisted. This is a tendency we must recognise, watch and resist. We need to strengthen our own links as movements.

Equal opportunities for exchange

Academics have their international conferences, professionals their training opportunities and workshops. People on the other side of the counter, both from the same and from different movements, need opportunities and support to get together, exchange information, share experience, recognise the overlaps between them and learn each others' lessons. This is true at local, regional, national and international levels.

FINALLY

Earlier I stressed the need for both a changed culture and adequate funding if user involvement is to flourish. So far in the modern history of British welfare these two key components, an empowering culture and adequate resources, have rarely both been present at the same time. In the 1960s and early 1970s when there was money for expansion, welfare's paternalistic culture was dominant and unchallenged. Now in the 1990s, when doors for cultural change are opening, the public purse is empty. But there are positive prospects for the future. Disabled people's, self-advocacy and service user organisations are growing in unprecedented numbers, strength and authority. They are developing models for user-led services which provide an alternative to the provider-led services we have known. Their critiques undermine the old orthodoxies. Nurturing these three developments must be our priority. One day there will again be resources for public services. Then when that day dawns we will be better placed than ever before to enable people's involvement and ensure their independent living. That's where the hope lies.

Working Together (1):
The Expression of Choice

JENNY MORRIS

While I spend most of my working life doing research and consultancy which aims to increase the control that users of public services have over those services, I also spend most of my private life doing everything I can to avoid being a user of services myself. Why is this?

I started off my life as a disabled person ten years ago, using public services such as home helps, my local GP, and so on, but I've gradually withdrawn more and more from doing so. This is primarily because my needs were not being met by the kind of services which were provided.

However, the practical difficulties caused by this kind of situation are in some ways not the major problem. I just cannot cope with the way that when I try to get my needs met, the reaction of service providers turns me into an angry, upset cripple with a chip on her shoulder.

Service providers all too often behave as if the users of their services are undeserving, demanding supplicants. I have come across this situation time and again in the research that I'm currently doing on disabled people who use personal assistance services (Morris, 1993). Those who are forced to use local or health authority services tread a very fine line in trying to get their needs met without upsetting the people on whom they depend and at the same time without being turned into angry ungrateful complainers.

What this research has also brought home to me is the way that user control in the delivery of services is a civil rights issue. We're not talking about an optional extra here. We are talking about something which is absolutely necessary if people are to live a reasonable quality of life. I go into people's homes and listen to stories which remind me of Terry Waite's description of what it's like to be a hostage. To be shut away, not listened to, your life devalued, and for some people to have no concept of how such a situation can ever end.

When the services that are provided don't address your actual needs, and when you are made to feel such an unreasonable, peculiar person if you point this out, the message you receive is that your life is worth little or nothing.

Unless those who require personal assistance are enabled to have control over how that assistance is provided, the institutionalisation of residential care will merely be replaced by institutionalisation within the community.

Some people argue that concepts of "user control" or "user empowerment" are only applicable to a minority of people, the assumption being that some people's impairments mean that they are not capable of exerting control over their lives. This argument relies on a very narrow definition of the concept of control. All human beings, whatever the nature and level of their impairment, are able to express choices in terms of what makes them happy and what makes them sad, what gives them pleasure and what causes pain.

Services should facilitate the expression of choice and in this way people would be empowered to achieve a better quality of life. Instead, we have a history of service provision based on so-called "experts" expressing choices on our behalf. It is this silencing of our voices which disables us rather than our physical, sensory or intellectual impairments.

User involvement in decisions about services is an idea whose time has not only come, but is long overdue. Over the last ten years or so, those people who use public services have come together in various contexts - as small groups, local organisations and a national movement - to insist that our voices are heard.

We also recognise that we have important allies amongst providers of services, and other professionals. All political and social movements need allies and it is crucial for users of services to be able to come together, on an equal basis, with those service providers who wish to further our interests.

What makes such a working together easier is that in many situations, people who provide services are, at some point in their lives, also users of services. We all need empowering against insensitive bureaucracies, driven by their own priorities, acting as methods of social control. We would all benefit from services whose prime aim is to increase the quality of and people's control over their own lives.

Part Two:
User-Led Initiatives

Access, Equal Opportunities and Anti-Discrimination Legislation: The Need for Organisations of Disabled People

LORRAINE GRADWELL

INTRODUCTION

The prevailing concepts and terminology around "service users" are very easily accepted as referring exclusively to disabled people. But non-disabled people are also service users. They use shops, hotels, banks, schools, travel agents, any or all of these service providers and more. In terms of "using" or accessing some of these services they may have satisfactory experiences. In other situations they have complaints to make, maybe action to take - even threats of litigation.

Consider - how do non-disabled people influence these services? Does the bank talk about "empowering" them? Does the travel agent invite them to comment on their proposed review of services - by a closing date which means if they don't respond tomorrow they have no chance of being heard? Does the local supermarket propose advocacy to help them understand what they are about? Of course not. At the end of the day, they "vote with their feet". They go elsewhere, and they take their money with them.

Consider again - how do disabled people "vote with their feet" when they are not the people buying the services? Where is our power? The plain truth is that the power to influence remains with the people who buy the service, and this is the crux of the matter. The people who "buy" the services influence what is on offer - they influence the funding of services and the allocation of resources. To talk about "empowering" service users is a nonsense without a commitment by the people in control to relinquish personal and organisational power over those very services.

As long as the professionals hold on to this power, there will be little hope of useful change. So disabled people need to form their own organisations - organisation *of*, not *for*, disabled people - to deal with the issues that most directly affect them, and challenge the existing structures of power.

THE GREATER MANCHESTER COALITION OF DISABLED PEOPLE

In the organisation I work for - the Greater Manchester Coalition of Disabled People (the Coalition) - the issues of access, discrimination, and equal opportunities are central to our activities. For many organisations these issues are desirable, but optional - how many job adverts do you see which state "We regret our premises are not wheelchair accessible"? Not an option for disabled people's organisations!

Firstly, a little bit of recent history - the Greater Manchester Coalition of Disabled People was initiated at a public meeting at County Hall in Manchester in 1984. This meeting was called "Strategies for a Coalition" and was attended by about 70 people who agreed that a Coalition of Disabled People should be set up, and nominated a steering group to make progress. The Inaugural Meeting was held in 1985 and by the end of 1986 there were three disabled people working for the Coalition.

Those three people are still working for the Coalition; we now have three other staff members and are currently recruiting two more. The organisation works through a management committee (the Executive Council) which is made up of disabled people only, so the work of the Coalition is planned, informed, and carried out by disabled people.

It is impossible here to cover the range of activities and issues addressed by the Coalition so I will take a few areas of work which are representative of what we do and try to demonstrate how we tackle discrimination and the lack of access and equal opportunities.

Employment

In terms of our day to day practices the Coalition only employs disabled people. The provision of access to the workplace is not an option for us and we are committed to working in flexible ways which do not discriminate. We have hosted work placements for disabled students, and will not hold any meetings in inaccessible venues.

The Coalition has been involved in campaigns and initiatives around employment. For example when the government's Disablement Advisory Service refused to provide sign language support for a Coalition employee we took it up with the Department of Employment and had the matter mentioned in the House of Commons. The Disablement Advisory Service is currently reviewing the provision they offer.

When Manchester City Council was setting up its Equal Opportunities Unit in the early days of the Coalition, Coalition representatives were among those who insisted, in the face of initial local authority opposition, that only disabled people were recruited. We believe that these were the first ever "disabled people only" job adverts.

Through the Disability Action Training project the Coalition delivers consultancy and training on employment policies and practices to commercial businesses, local and health authority bodies, to voluntary organisations and to disabled people themselves. All Coalition trainers are disabled people.

The Arts

The Coalition administers a small grant to make amateur theatres accessible, but there is quite a low take-up for this because the Coalition insists on full access being provided. Most projects are looking to "improve" access, or are creating two theatres from one and only making one of the new theatres accessible.

When the Carnegie Council wanted to stage a prestigious national arts conference called "Artability" at the Palace Theatre in Manchester, the Coalition fronted the opposition to the event though it was organised by the British Council of Organisations of Disabled People. Artability was being held at a theatre with limited access. And the organisers said they were doing this to highlight the problems of inaccessibility! With local and national organisations threatening to demonstrate if the conference went ahead, the Carnegie Council called off the event.

Another demonstration in which the Coalition was involved took place outside the local Granada television studio, in support of a disabled actor who had been unfairly turned down for the part of a disabled man in a children's programme, and a non-disabled actor used instead.

Discussion / analysis of issues

All Coalition policies and activities are informed by wide consultation and discussion of issues either through the Executive Council meetings, through sub-group meetings, through the regular Coalition open meetings or through the magazine *Coalition*. This appears quarterly and articles by both disabled and non-disabled people are used, although by far the greater number are by disabled people writing about issues relevant to the movement. *Coalition* is free to all full members in either text, braille, or on tape.

Supporting other organisations

The Coalition has worked with many organisations to support activities which are in line with Coalition aims. They may be disabled people's organisations, such as Rochdale and District Disability Action Group with whom we have worked closely on transport issues and on making funding applications, or other types of voluntary organisations such as Salford Law Centre, who were supporting people attending a day centre in their complaints to the local authority about changes in service provision which took place with no consultation.

Self-organisation

The Coalition is a disabled people's organisation - we decide our priorities, we decide how we will tackle them, we set our own agenda. Naturally we have funding constraints and we are limited by numbers: six or eight workers can only do so much. Nevertheless, simply by continuing to exist the Coalition sets models of good practice in terms of employing disabled people, in terms of constantly trying to make the organisation and its activities accessible to all disabled people, and in terms of identifying and tackling discrimination inside the Coalition as well as outside.

WHY ARE ORGANISATIONS LIKE THE COALITION IMPORTANT?

The Coalition is important because it was set up, and is controlled, by disabled people. The medical model of disability, which says that disability is a personal tragedy with which the individual must learn to cope, is rejected and replaced with the social model, which says that society should take account of the needs of disabled people. Needless to say, the overwhelming majority of services for disabled people are based firmly on the medical model. This means that there is a constant and consistent questioning of existing structures which, supposedly there to "help" us, actually oppress us and discriminate against us.

Organisations such as the Coalition accept self-definition of disability, rather than a medical "diagnostic" definition of whether or not a person is disabled. No doctor's note is needed to join the

Coalition! Disabled people's own organisations, like the Coalition, subscribe to the theory of independence, not "care" - whether in the community or not. This is vitally important to disabled people and the distinction between care and independence is not given enough prominence. From the point of view of a non-disabled person the notion of "care" may seem helpful and even attractive: to a disabled person it has connotations of dependence and lack of control, issues which the disabled people's movement seeks to address.

The disabled people's movement has many member organisations which depart from the traditional model of addressing specific issues, or comprising people of a particular type of impairment. The Coalition is one such generic organisation; it is not specific to either impairment or issue, neither does it relate to any one local or health authority. These facts enable the Coalition to take a step back and adopt a more overall view of disability issues. In terms of representativeness and accountability, the Coalition was set up by disabled people; it is run by, and employs only, disabled people; only disabled people can be full voting members. Whilst recognising the constant need to widen the representation of black disabled people, disabled women, gay and lesbian disabled people, and other under-represented groups, nevertheless the Coalition is still an organisation of disabled people.

As well as rejecting the medical model of disability, the Coalition rejects the power and control that charities have over the lives of disabled people, to the extent that the Coalition has taken the decision not to register as a charity. Charities have traditionally "looked after" disabled people, ensuring that they live, learn, and work in segregated institutions - "for their own good". More and more, disabled people are rejecting this approach and are challenging the big charities to stop raising money in order to oppress us in the name of do-gooding. In terms of financial implications, the Coalition's decision not to be a charity has meant a five year "discussion" with the Inland Revenue about the organisation's status in relation to paying corporation tax, but the current situation is that, whilst not being a registered charity, the Coalition nevertheless is exempt from paying corporation tax because it has charitable aims as defined by the Charity Commissioners. Discussions continue with our legal advisors!

Simply through the fact that it exists the Coalition proves that disabled people can organise, campaign, can be employers and employees. Disabled people can analyse and address the issues - we do not have to be passive, dependent recipients of care. Furthermore, *because* it exists the Coalition challenges and confronts the traditional ways of working, of informing and supporting people - ways that usually exclude disabled people. As they grow and develop, organisations such as the Coalition provide the space and opportunity for disabled people to build and share their skills as employers, as campaigners, skills in community development and outreach work, as speakers and facilitators at conferences and workshops. These are not areas of activity which are traditionally open to disabled people.

Disabled people's own organisations are important for many reasons, some of which have been outlined. They are important because of the work they do and the ways in which they do that work, but also because - simply by existing - they challenge the status quo. In many other organisations access and equality will be addressed to varying degrees: for our own organisations they are simply not negotiable.

Advocacy and Service Brokerage for Disabled People

DAVE MORRIS

INTRODUCTION

Disabled people do not need advocacy because they have impairments, but because they have been systematically disenfranchised from the constituency of ordinary living options by society.

"User-centred" is one of the "buzz words" of community care, along with care management, case management, service brokerage, advocacy and so on. However, giving users of services a real voice in the way they are delivered entails a massive cultural change within the service system, away from paternalism and control towards freedom, accountability and respect for individual rights.

Change is always difficult and often threatening, particularly when it involves transferring power. If the rhetoric of the National Health Service and Community Care Act is to be truly implemented, then it does involve divesting professionals of some of their power and giving it back to users. It also means a shift in status away from controlling experts, to expert consultants. There are dangers implicit in this threat to the status quo. There is a compelling force which guides the hand of the system to mutate into a reflection of itself. Social workers become case managers, negative power relationships remain intact and service users remain on the outside, treated as a commodity in an internal market where the brokers' contact with users is through complicated assessment forms and laptop computers.

Service users, however, are individuals with hopes and aspirations, wants and needs, expectations and responsibilities, loves and hates, fears and problems. We are not stereotypes who will respond automatically to neat labels, or fit snugly into pre-arranged packages. In the internal market the commodity is human, and difficult to assess, process and package.

It is easy to use terms such as user involvement and needs-led. It is more difficult to change practice so that it reflects those core concepts.

Advocacy is a facilitating part of the interface between changes in how the service system sees itself, or at least, how it should be seeing itself, the slow and often uncomfortable removal of the dusty robes of professionalism and power; and the beginnings of the empowerment of disabled people, the move away from passivity and care towards real autonomy, choice and control. Advocacy should be about enabling a quiet revolution to take place.

CHOICE is an independent, rights-based advocacy organisation administered and controlled by disabled people which is working at the cutting edge of this interface.

CHOICE AND CASE MANAGEMENT

CHOICE started life as the Case Manager Project
operating in Camden and Islington between 1986 and
1988, supported by the King's Fund. It was designed
to provide an innovative user-led model of working
which would help disabled people in getting packages
of services to meet a range of needs, that would be as
good as possible in terms of meeting the disabled
person's wishes, and given that the services existed.

The project was seen as necessary because the
experience of its founders, working in a spinal
injuries unit, was that many disabled people were
often unclear about what services were available, who
provided them, who was eligible for them, the route
that had to be taken to them and where to find this
information about them. It was proposed that a model
of working based on the idea of "case management", a
method of services provision then commonly
operating in North America but new and innovative
in the United Kingdom, could positively assist
disabled people achieve better, more coordinated and
more needs-based services.

Central to the objectives of this initial project was
that it would be "user oriented" and aim to give
disabled people the same kind of say in running their
lives as the rest of the population. The project
therefore had to be independent of any service
provision, hold no budget, not be solely funded either
by a health or local authority and most importantly,
led by disabled people.

The project aimed to give disabled people access to a
service which was:

- a single entry point to the whole system of services, where one worker would work with the person;

- accountable to the service user and not the service system;

- a way of gathering, together with the person, an holistic assessment of all needs;

- able to draw up a clear written plan of action with the person;

- able to coordinate individually tailored packages of support which would be monitored, and changed accordingly;

- a source of independent advocacy, where one worker could both represent the person and negotiate between different community services;

- a source of feeding back to planners the real needs and experiences of users across the whole network of community services.

The Case Manager Project proved that this model of working was successful, and that there was a demand from disabled people and people working within the system for the kind of independent service provided. At the end of the project therefore, CHOICE was formed as a voluntary organisation with charitable status, with a remit to replicate the project in other areas of the United Kingdom, providing consultation for people interested in developing similar services and training in the model of working. One of the fundamental criteria for the new organisation was that it would be managed and administered by disabled people.

In late 1989 a CHOICE service was set up in the London Borough of Barnet, funded in part by the local Social Services and in part by the Health Authority, and in late 1991 a CHOICE project was set up in the London Borough of Hackney.

EMPOWERMENT, SELF-ADVOCACY AND CONTROL

CHOICE's way of working has from the outset been designed to be flexible and responsive to the needs and wishes of the users of its service. CHOICE's model is a living one and has inevitably developed considerably since its inception, reflecting the growth of the disability movement itself and the on-going dialogue about disability issues. CHOICE no longer views itself as a "case management service", although recognising that much of its essence derives from practices implicit in the case management approach. CHOICE has endeavoured to build on this essence to provide a way of working which is about the empowerment of disabled people, self-advocacy and control.

Nationally CHOICE provides its consultancy services to a wide range of organisations both statutory and voluntary, and has become an acknowledged expert and leader in the field of user consultation and involvement in services, complaints procedures, advocacy and community care. CHOICE is also respected as a valuable source of training for professional advocates, "case managers" or "service brokers".

CHOICE is part of the wider movement of disabled people fighting for true equality of opportunity. Impairment must be seen as part of society's diversity, and disabled people a disadvantaged group analogous to other "minorities". CHOICE's model of working in direct partnership with individuals means that it is not itself a campaigning organisation or pressure group. It works in a way which is non-confrontational and aims to articulate the needs and wants of disabled people using the service in a progressive positive way. However the organisation holds a number of basic principles within which it works, and asks both service providers and service users to recognise and respect these.

Physical and intellectual difference is a normal fact of life and disabled people have the same basic human rights as anyone else. In a society which regards itself as humane and civilised no-one should have to accept an inferior quality of life simply as a result of having an impairment. CHOICE therefore challenges negative attitudes about impairment, be they explicit or hidden, and whether held by users of services or service providers. The organisation is well aware of the fact that we do not live in an ideal world, and places great emphasis upon dialogue and consultation as a positive response to this challenge.

It has to be accepted that the major handicap faced by disabled people derives not from the fact of a particular impairment, but from the attitudes of society towards impairment and the inappropriateness of many services offered to disabled people. This is exemplified by the low priority traditionally given to disabled people when resources are allocated, leading to the marginalisation of disabled people.

The general experience of disabled people is of a
society which often considers us as being abnormal,
unable and to a large extent invalid. Such attitudes
engender widespread prejudice and discrimination in
all spheres of our lives, resulting in limited
opportunities in living, education, employment,
leisure, transport, personal relationships and so on.
Such attitudes engender feelings among many
disabled people of being considered as second-class,
and lead to many disabled people having low self-
esteem, becoming passive recipients of "care" and
setting extremely low horizons for individual
development.

FACILITATING EQUALITY

Disabled people who require physical support in
everyday living should have the right to determine
and control their own living environment, have a lifestyle not inequitably hampered by the medical fact of
a disability, the right to personal fulfilment and to the
same hopes and aspirations as anybody else. The
experience of the independent living movement shows
that the great majority of such disabled people are
fully able to live on a basis equal to that of their non-
disabled counterparts, contributing to the community
in social and economic terms, given the availability of
appropriate facilities and support structures.

In relation to services which disabled people use,
CHOICE's remit is to work towards the development
and resourcing of structures which facilitate the
greatest possible level of choice, independence,
spontaneity, self-determination and control in living.
Such services should regard their responsiveness to
user-defined need as one of the most important
criteria in evaluating their performance.

Disabled service users and their representatives must be fully involved in the planning and delivery of the services they want and need. This requires that they be fully informed of the availability of services, that there are effective structures for consulting disabled people, that information is freely available, that disabled people have access to independent representation if they so wish. Not only should disabled people be able to make their own decisions about issues directly affecting their lives - they must also be allowed to make mistakes and take risks. Since no two people are alike, it is impossible to determine the effect of a particular impairment on any particular individual. For this reason, disabled people must be allowed to define their own limitations and abilities and assess their own needs.

CHOICE acknowledges that there are sections of society other than disabled people who do not enjoy equal rights. However this is no reason for compromise, and in the course of exercising its functions as both an advocacy organisation for individual users, and as an instrument for communicating users' experiences of services (or the lack thereof), CHOICE will continue to work on behalf of its users and disabled people in general for nothing less than complete equality.

Personal Assistance Schemes Under the Control of Disabled People: A Practical Guide

JANE CAMPBELL

CONTROLLING MY BODY

Over recent years disabled people have expressed an increasing desire to control their own lives.

This is seen in examples of disabled people forming and controlling their own organisations and leading their own campaign. The birth of the Spinal Injuries' Association in 1974, the arrival on the scene of the British Council of Organisations of Disabled People in 1981 and the campaign for a Civil Rights Bill from 1989 onward, are some of the many examples of such groups' self-determination. These and many other initiatives led by disabled people are each characterised by common ingredients: disabled people working together under the banner of human rights, to take control of what happens in their lives.

Northern Europe has a tradition of state welfare, but doubts are now being expressed about the philosophy behind most schemes. "Special housing", "special schools", "special transport" do not meet the aspirations of disabled people wanting to be full integrated members of the community. Disabled people wish to choose where they live, and as far as possible use the same facilities as everyone else. We have been accused of being "unreasonable", "selfish", "ungrateful" and "unreal". Wanting to "work and play" like everyone else is simply the aspiration of a "wealthy, articulate, assertive and intelligent minority". Realising such expectations, some say, would be at the expense of the less confident, the less able, the less secure.

We would challenge such undermining views. Control over what happens in our lives lies at the very heart of what we disabled people claim for ourselves. In response to criticism, we suggest that being in control of what happens in your life increases security because this means being less vulnerable to the dictates of others. These struggles for independence focus on specific issues: the most significant is control over the daily personal assistance we need in order to get up, go to bed, eat and get about.

Personal care is one of the earliest activities in which a child learns to become independent. Yet it is an area which few physically dependent disabled people get the chance to control. To be dependent on the control of someone else in the care of one's own body is to renounce a great deal of personal autonomy. Self management of personal care is critical to a sense of self worth and wellbeing.

Disabled people live in a world which has long excluded them from everyday life. We are discriminated against environmentally, attitudinally and through social systems. Disabled people are not expected to be active citizens. We are not part of mainstream educational, employment, or social activities. We are defined as largely individual physical or mental problems requiring "help" or "care".

We do not agree with this view. Organisations of disabled people are speaking out against such assumptions and working for change. Organising as a lobby is the only constructive way forward. We cannot leave it to others. We must involve ourselves in independent living: by doing so, we will never look back.

PERSONAL ASSISTANTS

Having control over the recruitment, selection and management of personal assistants (you may know them better as carers or helpers) is vital in maintaining maximum control over your life. Having tried several different types of care scheme, I have found from experience that the one which gives me the most freedom is the one which I am responsible for running myself.

Becoming an employer with responsibility for managing several full or part-time staff is a daunting prospect for anyone. If you are a disabled person, who has lived for years receiving "care" from some statutory agency, dishing it out on a daily basis without consulting you, it can seem an impossible task. It is not, however, as difficult as it first appears. Do not despair. There is a lot of useful guidance available from disabled people who are old hands at the whole business.

MAKE A LIST

Your first task is to find the right people for the job. Make a thorough list of the hours and tasks that you require, to give you *all* the help you need for the life you want to lead. This will form the basis of the job description(s), the advertisement, the interview questions and the final contract of employment.

Advertisements should state clearly that good pay is being offered, followed by the hours required and then a short *positive* description of the work to be done. Place it in local shop windows, the nearest job centre and the local papers, which are all fairly cheap. It is not much use advertising in national newspapers and magazines unless you are offering full-time work and/or accommodation. Notice boards in local sixth form colleges, polytechnics or adult education institutes give a high response to this type of advert, and are a cheap option.

A good response rate often depend on where you live. For instance, it is far harder to recruit in rural areas than in a university town teeming with students needing part-time work to boost their grants.

There is no cut and dried formula for the successful recruitment of personal assistants. It is very much about individual taste. You will certainly need to get on well with them (and vice-versa), as you are going to be spending several hours a day in each other's company. If someone gets on your nerves after a ten minute interview, consider carefully whether you have any real chance of getting on with them in the long term. Don't feel you have to take the first person who comes along.

There are important questions and information to be shared at the interview stage that will assist a successful future employer/employee relationship. Firstly, at the interview you should be very clear

about the sort of assistance you will require. Keep
asking for feedback so you can determine whether
you have been understood. It is useful to have
someone with you who has been through the process
of recruiting personal assistants on your first few
attempts.

Once an assistant is working for you, it is not a good
idea to try and form great friendships, because this
can make it difficult to maintain the control and
authority sometimes required. But it is important
that you relate on a basis whereby each party feels
comfortable and can communicate well.

The Trial Period

Always have a trial period of four to six weeks. At the
end of this, you may decide that things are not
working out and the employment can be terminated.
Even if things are going well, use the end of the trial
period to have a proper, honest review where you and
your personal assistant have the space to discuss
difficulties and, most importantly, the positive
aspects of the work. This "staff appraisal" (never
forget your management jargon) should be conducted
at three or six monthly intervals throughout the
employment. It gives a "definite" time when both
parties can get things off their chests.

It is important not to fall into a behaviour pattern of
being overly grateful for help given. It is all too easy
to allow your assistant to become the main decision-
maker - dare I say it, the "carer" - especially if this
has been your main method of operating for years. It
can feel secure and provide comfort, but is
nonetheless disempowering and wrong for both
concerned. At the same time, you should always be

ready to praise and value the work of your assistant, when appropriate. No employee will perform effectively unless they receive some positive feedback about their work.

The Extra Half Hour

For good working relations, being clear and sticking to agreed employment conditions is vital. According to American research carried out on personal assistants, one of the main reasons for leaving was that they didn't know when they were "off duty" or would be required to work "the extra half hour".

Working conditions should be clearly agreed and written into a contract that both parties sign. This can be a simple affair and should include whether you want them to be responsible for their tax and national insurance contributions as a self-employed person, or whether you will be responsible for that as well as statutory sick pay and holiday pay. The latter entails more work, but is becoming increasingly favoured by tax inspectors, who often require the employer to give evidence of their assistant's self-employed status. This could be their Schedule D number or a notice of self-employment given out by the local tax office. The Disablement Income Group has a simple guide book to Pay As You Earn and National Insurance Contributions for personal assistant users, which demonstrates the ease of the procedure (Dunne, 1992).

Employer's liability insurance is the other important responsibility of the disabled person who employs their own personal assistant. If your assistant has an accident when assisting you, then you are liable. Find a domestic insurance policy that covers this under a section referring to "servants". If your policy covers the situation, it is still worth asking for confirmation in writing. Some companies have asked for a small extra premium, but this is preferable to being sued for millions!

Recruiting and managing personal assistants becomes easier as time passes. Eventually it becomes second nature, and you develop such expertise that you know who is going to be suitable within the first few minutes of meeting. Over time you can also build up a pool of people who may no longer be regularly working with you, but are willing, even eager, to cover the odd emergency or holiday.

The *Source Book Towards Independent Living* published by Hampshire Centre for Independent Living (1987) is a very useful and thorough publication, giving lots of advice and examples of job descriptions, contracts, letters to interviewees, etc.

BALANCE OF POWER

Many disabled people find it hard to ask for what they really need in an assertive way that will command a positive response. We are so concerned not to fit the stereotype of being demanding or having a chip on the shoulder that we revert to apologetic requests which confuse the crucial balance of power. Keep in mind that you have just the same rights as anyone else to choose how you live your daily life.

Compare yourself to your family, friends and neighbours. If you are enjoying a similar lifestyle through personal assistants, then you know you are enjoying equality of opportunity - you don't have to be grateful! After all, you are paying for the service and should therefore behave in a professional manner which is directive but fair.

Working Together (2): Quality Action Groups

Mary Pannett, Paul Blake, Jay Lewis, Ruth Cochrane and Peter Allen

Introduction

The Avenue Resource Centre in the London Borough of Newham operates by attempting to find activities, mainly in the community, suitable for people with learning disabilities who previously lived in hospitals. Because health service managers were being increasingly asked to consider quality in their services and several people involved in services felt it was important, a quality action group was set up at the Centre.

The group started meeting in January 1990, and has met just under 20 times since then, with breaks over each summer. In October 1991 a number of new people joined the group, mainly because of staff changes. At first we had the same person chairing each meeting, but since October 1990 we have had a different person each time. This has given everyone a chance to be involved in this role.

What Is a Quality Action Group?

The main features are:

- A range of people involved in a service form a group and meet regularly.

- It is set up with the agreement and support of senior managers.

- The group always involves some service users and, where necessary, their advocates or supporters.

- The group's job is to look at and improve the quality of the service from the point of view of the people who use it.

- The group needs to find the best way of involving service users fully.

- The group collects information from outside and lets other people know what it is working on.

WHAT DOES IMPROVING QUALITY MEANS?

This involves a number of actions:

- Deciding what counts as quality:
    what are we trying to achieve?

- Looking at what actually happens:
    what are we achieving now?
    how does it compare with what we want for our service?

- Making changes:
    what most needs to be improved?
    how could we try to change it?
    where will we start?

- Evaluating:
    how well have we done?
    where do we go from here?

WHO DOES WHAT IN A QUALITY ACTION GROUP

Tasks and responsibilities are shared out as follows:

- *Group members*
    go to meetings
    agree what needs to be improved
    collect information
    think of ways to improve
    agree a plan of action
    put the plan into practice
    review progress.

- *The group leader*
    chairs the meetings
    makes sure everyone has their say
    makes it clear what has been decided
    makes sure that a record of decisions is kept.

- *The co-ordinator*
    helps groups get started
    supports one or more groups by:
        coming to some of the meetings
        helping the group leader plan the meetings
        giving the group leader feedback on how
            the group is going
        giving advice where needed
    keeps management informed about the
        work of the groups.

DIFFICULTIES

These are the problems that can arise:

- People being late or not being able to come.
  (Is this a high enough priority?)

- Trying to get more service users involved, wanting

a bigger group.
(People may not be used to contributing, or have difficulties in communicating.)

- People leaving.
  (Staff in services change, but the users do not.)

- Keeping the group going, new people coming in.
  (This requires a lot of energy and commitment.)

- Some issues can seem too big.
  (Is it really possible for this type of group to do more than comment on some of the *crunch* things?)

- Divided loyalties.
  (When you know why certain things are not likely to happen, but they are still big issues for stakeholders.)

WORKING TOGETHER

Deciding how to work together with a group needs preparation and imagination. Exercises which involve people in working together are useful. For example, in "Looking at Quality" members of the group have been asked to form into smaller groups of about five or six, and make posters using words, drawings and pictures cut out of magazines. This arouses great enthusiasm and some excellent representations of "quality", which are then discussed. The point of the exercise is that members have to define quality for themselves.

An exercise which we use to illustrate how to approach issues around quality and defining it, is to get people to talk and think about why they feel it is important to involve service users in services. We ask members to work in pairs, and give out large strips of paper and pens. Then we ask each of the pairs to write down what they think, and stick the papers on the wall. People are asked to walk round the room and see what others have written, and we spend a few minutes talking about things that are the same, or different.

Members enjoy non-traditional activities, such as taking polaroid pictures of people at meetings as a record. But at the same time the group has achieved a real input in improving the quality of services for the people who actually use them. This is of great value in furthering the work of the Avenue Resource Centre, which has acted as the major provider of day services for people with learning disabilities returning to Newham from hospitals outside the Borough. The Centre aims to match community facilities with the needs of people leaving hospital, and is, therefore, not a day centre but an outward looking service with an emphasis, naturally, on quality.

Part Three:
Provider-Led Initiatives

Consumers' Voices in Purchasing

INGRID BARKER, KATH MAINES AND LIZ WRIGHT

INTRODUCTION

For the first time in this country, a group of people who use mental health services are being funded to influence both the providers and the purchasers of local mental health services.

Newcastle Mental Health Consumer Group aims to make sure that people who use mental health services have a real say and significant role in the planning, development and monitoring of local mental health services. It provides a place for local people to share their personal experiences and views about mental health services. Members seek to promote actively the views of people who use mental health services to the people who provide and fund services.

CONTRACTING

One of the major reforms introduced by the National Health Service and Community Care Act is the split between purchasers and providers of services. Before the changes, health authorities directly managed some mental health services, and funded others such as those provided by local voluntary organisations through grants. Now each district health authority acts as a "purchaser" - it is given an allocation of money with which to buy all health services on behalf of the local population, acting as the agent of local

---

people. The nature of the services offered by a provider and the funding to be provided by the purchaser are set down in contracts or agreements between the two parties. The service providers may include voluntary organisations and units which have been previously managed by the health authority.

Each contract relates to the provision of one kind of service. It should cover the parties to the agreement; details of the service to be provided; who the service is for; how people will be referred to the service; the contract period; quality standards; monitoring and evaluation; equal opportunities and complaints procedures; the involvement of users and carers; the amount of payment due for the service; and procedures for resolving any dispute between the two parties.

In their role as purchaser, each health authority is expected to do the following:

- assess the needs of the population for health care
- prioritise use of money in relation to need
- decide what services will most appropriately meet those needs
- place contracts with providers for the right sort of services
- monitor the quality and effectiveness of those services.

NEWCASTLE MENTAL HEALTH CONSUMER GROUP

Newcastle Mental Health Consumer Group is made up of people who receive or have received mental health services, or who are close relatives or carers of people who receive these services. Membership is open to anybody who lives locally and fits one of these descriptions. The Group has been in existence since August 1990 and on a more formal basis since January 1991. Recently, more people have begun to get involved in the Group and it is hoped to increase the membership now it is well established. Some of the members have had experience of consumer involvement in voluntary or statutory organisations, others are new to this kind of involvement.

There is a management committee of up to fifteen, elected from the membership, which meets fortnightly to plan work and consider issues as they arise.

SETTING UP

The Group was drawn together by an independent consultant with skills in community development and a long experience of working to empower people locally. He was contracted by Newcastle Mental Health Trust to establish a group of users and carers to have input into services and increase their voice. At an early stage Newcastle District Health Authority undertook to fund the group jointly along with Newcastle Mental Health Trust.

During the first months of its existence, the Group concentrated on its own development. As with any such group, it was important for the members to share experiences with each other and develop trust among themselves. Thereafter, members could work together and generalise from individual experiences to benefit the work of the Group as a whole. Considerable time was spent in drawing up a constitution and agreeing objectives.

WORKING WITH BOTH PROVIDERS AND PURCHASERS

In a short time, the members of the Group became actively involved at all levels with both purchasers and providers locally. They work with Newcastle District Health Authority in conveying consumer views, to inform the authority in its purchasing of services and thus help determine the form of local mental health services. The Group is also in regular contact with people from all parts of Newcastle Mental Health Trust, the major provider of mental health services. This allows the Group to comment on existing services and influence the development of new ones, whilst working with Trust staff to increase active participation by consumers.

REGULAR CONTACT BETWEEN PURCHASERS AND CONSUMERS

At regular meetings with the Health Authority, generally through the contracts managers, matters relating to purchasing, user empowerment and quality of local services are addressed. Discussion is wide-ranging and includes agenda items set by both parties. The Health Authority has sought the views of the Group on specific matters - for instance the introduction of a "crisis card" for people who want to carry a record of their wishes in case they are in extreme distress and cannot consent to treatment, and the Group has raised questions for the Health Authority to investigate further - for example the benefits or drawbacks of the cook-chill method of preparing food. It has also been actively involved in drawing up a charter for users of local mental health services, along with representatives of the Mental Health Trust and the District Health Authority.

CONSUMERS AND CONTRACTING

Newcastle Mental Health Consumer Group works closely with Newcastle District Health Authority, contributing to the purchasing of mental health services in four main ways:

- needs assessment
- quality measures
- future planning
- monitoring contract performance.

Needs assessment.

Group members relate their own experiences and experiences of people they meet or know, in order to assist the Health Authority in assessing local need.

Quality measures

The Group has contributed greatly to the detail of contracts for mental health services between the Health Authority and local providers (mainly the Mental Health Trust), in suggesting clauses which they think will ensure good quality services.

It has also made suggestions about privacy, confidentiality, the provision of food and facilities relating to refreshments, social activities, patients' clothing, money, increased choice and accessibility of services etc. As well as addressing quality issues such as these, the Group is encouraging the inclusion of measures promoting increased consumer participation in running services. For example, one of the contracts for 1992-93 between the Trust and the Health Authority contains a provision for "patients councils" to be set up, and for a user-led social and recreation facility to be available for consumers of that service seven days a week.

Several other quality clauses have been included in
the 1992-93 contracts which arose out of discussions
between the Group and service providers and
purchasers, such as providing for every patient to
have access to tea and coffee on request, to have a
quiet place to see visitors, to have information about
aftercare and where to get help on discharge, the
introduction of crisis cards, a review of an incentive
scheme.

Future planning

A group called "Purchasing for People" meets
quarterly, convened by the Health Authority. It
comprises Consumer Group members, GPs,
community health council members and social
services planners. This forum aims to assess need
and plan services for the future. Group members
provide evidence relating to the needs of service
users, and give their views about the shape of future
services. The Group welcome the opportunity to be
involved at this stage of developing services that are
truly responsive and flexible to consumers in "crisis".
Members of Purchasing for People have visited
innovative schemes around the country to explore
alternative models of service provision.

Monitoring the performance of contracts

The Consumer Group is able to feed back information
to both providers and purchasers of services to help
them evaluate how a contract is being performed, and
they have shared in joint discussions to review
performance.

In order to comment on present or proposed contracts,
the Group members draw on their own personal
experiences of services, and the information they gain

from regular visits to services provided by the Trust. Members are visiting each Trust service in turn and intend to cover all eight contract areas. Their views are systematically recorded and related back to contracts managers as well as to managers within the Trust.

Money

The Consumer Group is funded by Newcastle Mental Health Trust and Newcastle District Health Authority. They finance an independent facilitator to support the Group three days a week, and also pay all fifteen members of the elected management committee a regular sum each month in recognition of their work. The constitution of the Consumer Group includes a commitment to the principle that people who use services and carers should receive payment for work carried out in a planning or advice giving capacity, or at any time when it feels their unique knowledge and expertise is necessary.

CONCLUSION

The Group undertakes a lot of hard work - that set out here is only part. The members are dedicated to making the Group work, and it also owes a great deal to the commitment and vision of people within Newcastle District Health Authority and Newcastle Mental Health Trust. In Newcastle things are changing: consumers are using new structures to make their voices heard and becoming increasingly involved in the planning and running of services.

Community Care and Assessment: The Birmingham Approach

BOB FINDLAY

INTRODUCTION

Birmingham Social Services Department is the largest in the country and therefore the introduction of the Children Act and National Health Service and Community Care Act has required a significant restructuring. Birmingham like most authorities is still trying to put its operation into place. Because of local circumstances, the first stage in moving towards community care was the development of a community care assessment form.

The Department's commitment to user involvement has mainly centred around developing user consultation frameworks such as the City Council's Community Care Special Action Project, rather than including user representation on committees. User consultation has taken a variety of forms, including listening to individual user's views on their own needs. This is the context from which the community care assessment form came into being.

THE HISTORICAL BACKGROUND

The history of the assessment form is relatively complex. City Council policy for elderly people and their carers, known as the "Agenda for Change", had stated that the existing assessment form, known as

72

CR6, should be replaced. Officers working with elderly people entered into a dialogue with other officers who were also addressing the issue of assessment because of the 1986 Disabled Persons Act. This requires a formal assessment to be made of people with disabilities including an assessment of carers' needs, listing agreed needs and giving a statement of services to be provided.

The dialogue began during 1990 and received fresh input from the publication of the National Health Service and Community Care Act. Section 47 requires an assessment for the provision of community care services, giving social services a lead role in designing community care arrangements through assessment and care/case management. Because of the existing interest and concern about assessment, Birmingham Social Services Department took this part of the Act up first.

It was not realised at the time, and only apparent now with hindsight, what implications this starting point would have in terms of fitting assessment into the overall framework of service delivery of community care. What we did was to start in the middle of the process, and this may result in problems when the two "ends" are developed.

A working group was established to review the existing form CR6 and develop a new assessment form. It was decided that the group would not be, in its initial stages at least, a multi-agency group but that widespread consultation would take place once a draft form had been developed. The decision to operate in this manner was based on the belief that the Department had to explore a number of internal agendas before it would be able to address external ones.

The exclusion of external staff also meant the non-representation of users: involvement of users and representatives was to be addressed through the existing consultation process.

DESIGNING THE FORM

The original membership of the working party sought initially to update the content of the CR6 form and bring it into line with the legislation requirements as well as existing policy. Exploring the basic methodology of undertaking assessments was not a central issue. It was only when two officers from the Policy, Performance and Review section, concerned with disability issues, were invited to join the working group and expressed particular concern over how assessment procedures traditionally used a medical or personal tragedy approach towards disability, that the question was raised. The outcome of such approaches is a focus on "needs" as determined by medically based evaluations of functional limitations associated with an individual's particular condition or impairment. This, it was argued, produced narrow, negative and often oppressive interpretations of an individual's needs.

Discussions around this led to a critique of the methodologies used in developing assessments and consideration of ways of designing a form which would assist in changing assessment procedures and promote a culture of working with people. We wanted to remove the expectations and assumptions imposed by seeing "needs" as something generated by individuals "having something wrong with them", and instead enable individuals to identify the concerns and needs they had arising from their present lifestyles. This means addressing "needs" in terms of creating opportunities, dismantling barriers, improving the quality of support and ensuring appropriate service delivery. The idea of "needs" within this context takes on a different feel.

Given the nature of the Department and the demands of the legislation, it was recognised that to break completely from an "individualised model" would be extremely difficult and ultimately determined by how users influenced policies and service provision.

So the first task was to establish what the form should set out to do, which was to:

• provide a format by which information about a person's community care needs could be obtained in a consumer friendly and ethnically appropriate way;

• be appropriate for assessing all adults, not only elderly people, and therefore avoid being age or disability specific;

• assess the carer's needs separately, and list them;

• keep the focus of assessment of need separate from the focus of listing service provision;

• provide a statement of need and a statement of services to be provided.

It was agreed that the form design should take a modular format, so that each section could if necessary:

- stand alone
- be transferred on completion to other service sections providing particular services.

The resulting form therefore consisted of sections covering:

- initial information required
- social and community support
- home environment
- personal profile
- health
- daily living activities
- benefit entitlement
- carer/supporter details
- identified needs.

THE APPROACH TO ASSESSMENT

Within the framework of designing and piloting the form, the working group were aware of the necessity of ensuring that both the issue of equal opportunities and user empowerment were taken on board. Shifting the form's emphasis away from a medicalised perception of need towards a social one was a vital component of this process.

The "daily living activities" section demonstrates best the issues here. Previously, this section would have been broken down into questions relating to an individual's functional loss in undertaking specific tasks. The Office of Population Censuses and Surveys has developed this style of assessment and has been criticised for it (Oliver, 1990). What we tried to do was to move away from circumscribing people through narrow closed questions such as "Do you have difficulties dressing yourself?" We wanted the people who were being assessed to help establish the agenda. The introduction to the section thus says:

> "Do you have any needs or concerns arising from your daily living activities? These might include for example: needing someone to help you, the length of time it takes to do things, particular activities that are difficult, lack of equipment, lack of opportunity to do certain things, unhappiness with existing help you have etc. Please give examples so we can have an overall picture."

The form moves through key periods of daily living and expects the person being assessed and the assessor to identify the issues together.

It must be noted that one of our teams saw the question and approach as "putting emphasis on what clients cannot do." The meaning of "cannot do" was not qualified. In my own field, that of disability, professionals remain utterly confused between seeing "disability" as negatively located within the individual and "disability" as the negative consequence of specific social relations. This is the reason for pointless demands that, for example, we "look at the ability not the disability" of a given individual. This approach may appear "positive" to those who advocate it, but in reality it is not so because it still defines disability as negatively located within the individual.

The question in the assessment form was not based on an expectation that the person would outline their entire lifestyle, but rather would target issues and concerns which would enable the assessor to discover where an intervention might be required, or the type of disabling barriers the person might need support to confront. In this sense, we were indeed seeking to address "what clients cannot do", but from within an enabling perspective.

Here, I believe, is the heart of the debate around "assessing community care needs". The overall task is to provide a framework to enable individuals to enter or remain within their communities and achieve a meaningful quality of life. The assessment form is therefore a tool to be employed by both the potential service user and the service provider. To act as a tool the form must be accessible, and users aware of their right to put it into operation.

USER INVOLVEMENT AND EMPOWERMENT

The assessment form is only part of the process, a cog in a very large wheel. The community care process relies initially on the ability of service providers to make known to potential users what is on offer. I believe this to be a major issue to which both government and local authorities have paid too little attention.

The expectations of various client groups, especially those who experience disability, have risen over the last decade. User involvement is no longer merely a question of "keeping people informed" about what is going on or "seeking an opinion". The ground is shifting towards the demand for recognised legal rights, greater choice and direct control over one's own life.

The notion of "need" itself is subject to debate as people with disabilities attack the dependency model which underpins most existing social policy. Should we speak of "needs" or "wants"? I believe there is a contradiction here. The dependency model means "needs" are prioritised over "wants" and the legal ramifications of not addressing "needs" have been clearly demonstrated by the court action against Hereford and Worcester Social Services Department, where an individual was granted leave to mount a High Court challenge on the grounds that the Council was acting illegally by refusing him the right to a full-time personal assistant. The action was to be taken under the Chronically Sick and Disabled Persons Act (1970) but was settled out of court.

With limited resources available to local authorities it is obvious that the debate around "rights" versus "resources" is going to be very much on the minds of both service users and service providers. At present there is little debate about how the issue of "rights" can and should be drawn into the processes of managing "resources". The philosophy of community care, despite all the political hype, maintains the dependency model and thus reinforces the "them and us" relationship between users and service providers. It is my view that the court action in Hereford and Worcester is an early indication that people are no longer prepared to be passive recipients of services, and will increasingly become ever more determined to ensure they have a direct say in what is being provided for them.

Local authorities cannot afford to adopt a knee-jerk reaction to this, to bury their heads in the sand and hope the issues will go away. The reality is that they won't. This means facing up to the consequences of working with people to "assess needs" and identifying the outcomes. Outdated procedures for undertaking assessments are more likely to produce conflicts and possible legal action than the adoption of procedures which enable both service providers and users to see step by step what the issues are, and to address them as they arise.

The assessment procedure must have a degree of autonomy from the rest of the community care process, but cannot be left in total isolation. To keep it completely outside creates two negative features: first, there is a great risk of raising false expectations among users if there is no relation to what can actually be delivered. This does not mean assessment must be governed by the resource implications, but at the same time we must avoid offering meaningless "blank cheques."

Second, it hinders the ability of service providers to use the information obtained through assessments to monitor take up of services, shortfall, modifications suggested by individuals etc. To improve the quality of services and ensure they are accountable, this type of information is of paramount importance. I am therefore convinced that only through "openness" and user involvement at all levels will local authorities avoid bloody legal battles with dissatisfied customers.

CREATING "OPENNESS" AND USER INVOLVEMENT

Much work has to be done to ensure that access points are appropriate and user-friendly: the culture around assessing "needs" requires a massive shift. It is therefore important for the assessment form to be seen by both users and professionals as a meaningful and useful tool. The terms "ownership" and "partnership" are not often used in relation to assessment, but for community care to succeed these concepts are essential.

Birmingham has sought to put the individual at the centre of its assessment process, and sees it as vital that both potential users and carers help shape service delivery. If the response to assessing "needs" is sufficiently flexible, people will be empowered rather than disempowered by their experiences. This approach will not only help to target issues for individuals, but can also reduce their feelings that "assessment" leads nowhere.

The community care assessment form is intended to open up dialogue and lay the basis for partnership between users and service providers. Users will be able to discuss what is possible and what is not with the assessors and care managers, setting agendas around their own particular care needs.

UNRESOLVED ISSUES

It is extremely difficult to divorce issues such as assessment from care management, or the provision of resources. So far the following distinct stages have been identified: access to services; assessment for service; care management; service delivery/purchase; and drawing up the community care strategy. In Birmingham we have begun to involve users in drawing up the community care strategy and piloting the assessment form, but only on an ad hoc basis. Concern has been expressed that as these stages are developed they may well impinge on others either just started or yet to come. Equally, stages such as the assessment form could be affected by events as yet unknown.

The urgent question now is how to ensure that the philosophy and approach which informed the development of the assessment form is carried through to all the other stages. The issue of user involvement is a key aspect of the answer.

POSTSCRIPT

Since this paper was first written I feel the Department has revised its approach to the "assessment process" and many of the fears indicated in the concluding paragraphs above have sadly become a reality.

Support for Disabled Elderly People from Ethnic Minority Groups

BETTY ASAFU-ADJAYE, MARIA-ANTONIA MANCHEGO-PELLANNE AND DEBORAH WHALL-ROBERTS

THE NATURE OF ETHNICITY

In the United Kingdom, the ethnic majority seems to find it difficult to understand that members of minority ethnic groups can and need to keep their own cultural identity, and if necessary be served in their own language. This requires understanding and good-will, but more fundamentally it is commitment at decision-making level which is necessary to generate and develop responsibility for the implementation of *equal rights to meet equal needs*.

SERVICES AVAILABLE TO DISABLED ELDERLY PEOPLE

There is widespread provision of specialised services for elderly people in the United Kingdom - primary health care, home care, home help, residential care, meals-on-wheels, day centres, luncheon clubs, holidays, respite care, support for carers, publicity information about services etc. Elderly people from the ethnic communities should also be recipients of the same services. Unfortunately this is not the common practice.

The Standing Conference of Ethnic Minority Senior Citizens is a registered charity working to facilitate and improve the provision of services among elderly

people of different ethnic backgrounds. We provide
support to our member groups by developing their
skills mainly through training tailored to their needs
and by facilitating access to funding. We are also
working for the improved co-ordination and
development of services to carers.

Demand has forced us to develop an over-the-
telephone referral service for social workers, hospital
social workers, voluntary and private sector agencies
and for workers and individuals in need of support
from a community group or person, for the provision
of services to elderly isolated and ill clients.

The Standing Conference of Ethnic Minority Senior
Citizens advocates that every elderly person has the
rights of choice, dignity, independence and security,
as integral and valued members of society, and to
equal enjoyment of these rights whatever the person's
cultural, religious and political background. There are
many factors which make services *unavailable,
insufficient* or *unsuitable* for the many elderly
communities we represent: languages, cultural
specifications, lack of knowledge of what is available,
prejudice etc. The problem is *not only lack of services,
but the suitability of and access to the services, and the
provision of information about them.*

From our contact with over 250 member groups
running day centres and luncheon clubs, and from
the information gathered when we evaluated their
work and provision of services to their clients, we
concluded that the care of disabled, deaf, blind and
mentally distressed people has to be one of the
targets for development by the organisation. These
groups are not being integrated in many of the

member groups, with only very few exceptions. A great number of people are not benefiting from services, leaving them isolated and unsupported. Group co-ordinators and community workers do not have the support of trained staff to deal with the requirements of people from disabled groups or develop the understanding and co-operation of able-bodied members of the community, and their willingness to share provision of services with them.

TRAINING PROJECTS

To equip the groups with trained workers in different areas of specialisation, we are developing training partnerships with voluntary organisations who have specialised knowledge of different areas of disability. Our first project, "The Care of Deaf People" in partnership with the Royal National Institute for Deaf People, provided training for community workers from 12 different ethnic groups, lasting for one year. This finished in June 1991 with the presentation of certificates. The second joint training session was attended by 20 community workers from Vietnamese groups in London. The training was conducted by deaf tutors with the help of Sign and Vietnamese full-time interpreters, in a five-week block with a final test to qualify for a certificate.

At the moment, we are implementing our third joint training project, this time in partnership with the Royal National Institute for Blind People. "The Care of Blind People" follows the same pattern as "The Care of Deaf People". After the completion of training, trainees return to their community groups to implement schemes for the care and support of their disabled clients and their carers.

One outcome of this commitment to ethnic disabled members of the community has been the appointment by the Royal National Institute for Deaf People of their first ever African, Afro-Caribbean, Asian and Ethnic Minorities Officer (South East Office), Deborah Whall-Roberts, employed to work solely with ethnic minority communities. This post has been funded by the Department of Health's section 64 grant, to identify, facilitate and enable ethnic minority groups to offer each other self-help and support, whilst making their specific needs known to service providers and professionals in the field of deafness.

The Standing Conference of Ethnic Minority Senior Citizens has helped, through the training programmes, to assess the availability of specialist services for deaf and hard-of-hearing people from the ethnic minority communities. Some non-deaf people tend to forget that "deaf" people are full members of society. They have equal rights, should be afforded equal respect and *must* be able to exercise equal opportunities. Due to the lack of interpreters, it is very difficult for ethnic minority deaf people to have the mode of communication of their choice. However, *all deaf people* have rights to equality of access to information and full participation in society.

In providing services, full account must be taken of deaf people from ethnic minority cultures, their experiences, their values, their rights and their opinions. Over the last 18 months, the Royal National Institute for Deaf People Officer has found that services provided for the ethnic minority deaf community are not adequate or sufficient. Because of lack of interpreters, some deaf people from various nationalities find it difficult to communicate with people who do not understand their religion, culture and traditions.

One of the more innovative projects initiated by the Royal National Institute for Deaf People and the Standing Conference of Ethnic Minority Senior Citizens was the application made to the "Opportunities for Volunteering" scheme for funding to train volunteers from ethnic minority groups to learn about deafness and gain a wider understanding of the needs of deaf people. This was jointly co-ordinated by the two organisations and took the form of a year's course.

The trainees took the information they learned on the course back to their community groups, and translated it from English into their own mother-tongue. They explained how deafness occurred, where deaf people can go for environmental aids, what help is available, who the particular social worker for the deaf is in their borough. They also took Hi-Kent Communication classes on sign language, so they could learn the basics of British Sign Language. The different nationalities from which the trainees came were West Indian, African, Asian, Chinese, Arab, Vietnamese, Spanish, French, Latin American, Armenian, East German, Greek and Turkish. The community groups are still linked with the Royal National Institute for Deaf People Officer, who provides support and help with queries, problems, new equipment, and information on environmental aids, as well as giving talks on deafness at open days etc.

AIMS AND OBJECTIVES

The aims and objectives of the projects can be stated as consumerism, advocacy, support to local organisations and improving the availability of appropriate statutory services:

- *Consumerism* : exploring possible mechanisms for consultations with consumers in the community, seeking to involve consumers and other people in the work of the Royal National Institute for Deaf People, and making local consultancy channels accessible to deaf ethnic minority people.

- *Advocacy*: in all its forms.

- *Local voluntary organisations*: devising means of support to enable them to function more effectively and improve their support for disabled people; and also to foster and develop regional associations.

- *Local authority services*: to press them to improve their services, through consultancies, undertaking reviews of existing services, and through the possibility of contract agreements to deliver appropriate services to meet the needs of deaf people from African, Afro-Caribbean, Asian and other ethnic minority communities.

We also aim to establish and make more links with other organisations which may be interested in setting up social club, youth club and luncheon club activities, where young and elderly deaf people from ethnic minorities can meet on a regular basis, or help them set up their own clubs and organisations and apply for funding.

NOTE

The material about the Royal National Institute for Deaf People initiatives in this chapter was supplied by Betty Asafu-Adjaye and Deborah Whall-Roberts.

Including Older People in Community Care Planning

JULIE BINGHAM, ANNE JAMES AND MARJORIE MAYO

INTRODUCTION

Both in Britain and beyond, there is increasing
understanding of the ways in which user
participation can enrich service planning, bringing
new possibilities for making services more
appropriate and more accountable. But the process of
developing user involvement also brings its own
dilemmas for service providers, dilemmas which need
to be recognised and faced if the outcome of user
participation is to be positive rather than frustrating
on all sides. In particular, service providers need to
recognise that user participation can and typically
does lead to increasing demands for public sector
provision, as well as increasing the potential for
voluntary contributions, mutual support and self-
help. This is a theme which has emerged both in
Britain and across national boundaries.

Furthermore, when users are involved in service
planning, they do not necessarily perceive the issues
which are most important to them in terms which fit
neatly in with departmental boundaries. So when
older people are consulted on community care
planning for instance, they can and do raise issues
which go beyond the remit of social services and the
National Health Service. The process of user
involvement needs to take account of these inter-
departmental concerns.

Finally, user involvement itself needs to be resourced. Even well established user groups such as the Oxford Pensioners' Action Group need additional resources, to enable them to develop their own agenda for community care, with the confidence that they were fully representing the views of all pensioners including housebound people, as well as their more active members.

THE OXFORDSHIRE APPROACH

User involvement of older people in community care planning in Oxfordshire had two strands in its first phase: the commitment of Oxfordshire pensioners to becoming actively involved from their own perspective, and the commitment of Oxfordshire Social Services as the planning authority. Oxfordshire's planning officers, who co-ordinated public consultation on the 1992-93 Community Care Plan, took as a starting point the view that older people can be both consulted and involved in community care planning in two ways: they can be involved in the planning of their own care or the care of someone close to them; or they can become involved in strategic planning, or both.

The National Health Service and Community Care Act and the guidance to local authorities that has been issued subsequently, require social service departments to make sure that people are fully involved in individual care planning and have the opportunity to contribute to strategic planning if they so wish. But to make this happen, some things need to change. Frequently at the moment service users and carers do not fit comfortably into the ways in which planning is constructed - and it is wrong to assume they should.

For the individual wishing to contribute to their personal care plan, the assessment and care management requirements of the Act and the guidance should help. Workers are required to agree with individuals and their carers the sort of package of care that would be most suitable, and to ensure the package is regularly reviewed so that it can be altered to suit altered circumstances. Care plans where agreed should be signed by both parties, and any disagreement about what services are offered or how they are offered should be recorded. But although there should be important potential benefits from these new procedures, as far as individuals and their carers are concerned, Oxfordshire Social Services recognised at an early stage in 1991 that the procedures would not be sufficient to address the issue of user involvement in strategic planning.

Whilst Social Services was working on ways of developing user consultation processes, at its end Oxford Pensioners' Action Group meanwhile was developing its own perspectives on user consultation on strategic planning. The Group wanted to develop a practice approach so that pensioners would be setting their own agenda for community care planning, rather than merely reacting to Social Services' definitions of the issues. And the Group wanted to be able to be confident that the organisation really was expressing the views of all pensioners, housebound people as well as the active pensioners who contributed at meetings.

THE OXFORDSHIRE PENSIONERS' ACTION GROUP SURVEY

One of the ways forward was a survey by the Oxford Pensioners' Action Group to explore pensioners' own perspectives on the issues involved in strategic

community care planning. The Group obtained a
grant from Charity Projects to carry out their own
survey of pensioners' views on the services which they
were receiving, together with their views on any gaps
in service provision. The questionnaire was designed
with the active involvement of the Group, and Group
members also carried out some of the interviews,
covering both individual service users (including
housebound people) and members of pensioners'
clubs.

The preliminary report of this survey was included in
Oxfordshire's 1992-93 Community Care Plan,
forming a users' contribution to services for elderly
people. This recognition of pensioners' perspectives
was in itself valued, demonstrating as it did
Oxfordshire's concern to build users' views into the
planning process.

The preliminary findings showed the following:

- Pensioners in the main are very active and
  involved in mutual support. Elderly people are the
  main carers both for themselves and for each
  other, within families and between neighbours.
  Overall, community care for the elderly is also
  community care by the elderly, to a considerable
  extent.

- Pensioners place great value on social and
  community activities such as lunch clubs, which
  tend to have longstanding membership. Clubs are
  attended mostly because of the company.

- Pensioners also value a range of other leisure and
  community activities, hobbies and interests.

Relevant services include community education
and leisure services for instance, not just health
and social services community care provision.

- Transport emerged as a major issue, both in terms
  of transport to and from health and social services
  provision, and in terms of transport to the wider
  range of social and community facilities.

These preliminary findings demonstrate precisely the
introductory point, that users' concerns do not
necessarily fit neatly into departmental boundaries.
Whilst elderly people in Oxfordshire are deeply
involved in community care issues, both as providers
and receivers of care, their definitions of their
concerns go far beyond those of health and social
services to include a wide range of leisure and
community facilities, which they see as centrally
related to their overall well being. In addition, the
survey demonstrated widespread concern about
material considerations, particularly focusing upon
the inadequacy of state pensions and the lack of
accessible information about the range of welfare
benefits. There were a disturbing number of cases
where individuals seemed not to be receiving benefits
to which they were entitled, cases which were
subsequently followed up with detailed welfare rights
information and advice.

In addition, the survey identified a number of issues
which were more specifically related to Social
Services' provision of community care. The common
thread here was the demand for increased levels of
service provision. There were virtually no complaints
about the services which were received; but there

were a considerable number of complaints about the need for more, especially for more home care. And Oxfordshire had just reorganised the home care service to concentrate on provision of personal care to those in greatest need! This relates back again to the introductory point about user participation and its potential impact in terms of increasing demand for services, as well as maximising voluntary contributions, and mutual support and self help.

There was also an issue around provision for black and minority ethnic clients, raising major questions about the accessibility and appropriateness of community care services in terms of equal opportunities. Other information sources make it clear that there *are* elder ethnic people who do need a range of services, but there are problems about both the accessibility and the appropriateness of these services. Here too there are potential resource implications.

The analysis of the survey was still being completed at the time of writing. Although the survey provided Oxford Pensioners' Action Group with valuable information which offered a basis for further consultation with older people in Oxfordshire, the process did have the disadvantage of being time-consuming, with results taking longer to obtain than had been anticipated: a point which users need to bear in mind when planning surveys like this.

Once analysis is completed, both the survey results and the group comments will be fed into community care planning in Oxfordshire, to develop a continuing dialogue with a view to creating adequate structures for older people to participate in planning and monitoring of care in the community, both in policy and practice.

SOCIAL SERVICES CONSULTATION

At the same time as the Oxford Pensioners' Action Group survey was taking place, Oxfordshire Social Services was also undertaking its own consultation in preparation for the publication of its community care plan. This took place between May and December 1991 and in total involved some 1500 people. The process incorporated both consultation with free standing user representative groups and also included the preliminary findings of the Oxfordshire Pensioners' Action Group survey.

The process was co-ordinated by the Social Services' community care planning team in partnership with operational staff in each of Oxfordshire Social Services' six divisions. The intended spin off from working through line management structures, developing consultation at very local levels, was to create ownership of the plan and planning by staff throughout the Social Services Department: this has largely been successfully achieved. Flourishing community care planning groups and forums now exist in most parts of the county, their focus being on local services and local issues.

Social Services and the Oxford Pensioners' Action Group both feel that the best consultation and involvement is that which is developed in partnership and is locally based. Consultation works best when people meet as equals, users and professionals together. A workshop on "Involving Older People in Community Care Planning" considered that older people should develop free standing groups, committees or structures such as the Pensioners' Action Group, rather than accept the practice which is all too common among service providers, that of co-opting individual users or carers on to existing planning groups. At best this is practice tokenism, and at worst an exploitation of the individual and an effective means of denying older people the right to express their own views, both individually and corporately, in their own way.

Outcomes

But a note of caution should be sounded. The Pensioners' Action Group is well established and well respected in Oxfordshire and their views are sought by the local authority and they are affiliated to national pensioners' groups. They have a European stance too: the Oxfordshire chair attends the European Pensioners' Parliament. But even such a well-established group as the Oxford Pensioners' Action Group has to ask itself on the basis of previous experiences "Will anything tangible actually happen when pensioners do voice their needs?"

Consultation systems can be merely a public relations exercise. For example the Thames Valley Police sent a speaker to one of the Pensioners' Action Group public meetings, who finished his talk by asking what pensioners would like from the police. They told him overwhelmingly that the meeting had made it clear that what they wanted was more "bobbies on the beat". Despite this request being widely reported in the local press, nothing has yet happened. It is no good saying to pensioners that changes take time to implement. The one thing that older people have not got is time.

Oxfordshire is only at the beginning of the process of consultation. It has a long way to go, as have other authorities and areas. However, what is emerging is the commitment by both those working in local authorities to implement care in the community policies and by older people themselves, to ensuring that older people's views *do* contribute to the way in which services are offered and that policies *are* implemented. In order to do this, new ways of involving older people and their carers in commenting on and planning for services need to be developed, so that each can give of their best and genuinely contribute both at an individual level and at a strategic level.

The Oxford Pensioners' Action Group however has reservations about how far this perspective is likely to be implemented in practice. How far will users' collective views actually be taken into account in strategic planning? What about the issue of increased home care provision for instance, where user groups are clearly pressing for additional resources to extend the present level of service provision? And how far will even individuals' views be taken into account when specific community care packages are drawn up for particular clients, if these clients begin to put additional pressure upon scarce resources? Or how far can social services develop effective mechanisms for liaison with other service providers, to collaborate on taking account of user perspectives on such issues as transport, community education and leisure provision to meet the needs of older people, for their well-being as a whole?

Concerns for individual elderly people remain too. What about the many old people living alone, unable to get out, about whom the services never hear? Or those who are afraid to criticise services in case they lose the service altogether?

Independent groups and organisations such as the Pensioners' Action Group need to be ready for the challenges ahead.

Involving Service Users in HIV Services in Hammersmith and Fulham Social Services Department

FENELLA TREVILLION

Involving service users in setting up services for people affected by HIV has always been an important element of Hammersmith and Fulham Social Services' strategy. At times this has been very useful, important and helpful both to service users and to the Department, but at other times mistakes have been made, the needs of service users possibly overlooked and they have become rather lost in the bureaucracy. I shall give some examples of different ways in which we have involved service users and identify some of the advantages and disadvantages of the mechanisms used before summarising what we have learned from these experiences.

HIV POLICY AND PRACTICE GROUP

This was a Departmental group that involved workers from a variety of different levels and divisions within the Department, and also had as part of its membership local service users and members of voluntary organisations. It was an "ideas and trouble shooting" group, chaired by the Deputy Director of the Department.

The HIV Policy and Practice Group was very successful in its time (the late 1980s) when there was tremendous uncertainty about what was the best way to set up services, but as the organisation changed, the usefulness of the Group changed also.

Disadvantages

Because of the predominance of council officers as Group members there was a problem with language, and "social services speak" was the dominant mode of conversation. The service users involved, who were members of voluntary organisations as well, found they had to learn a lot quickly, and as an organisation we didn't find many mechanisms for helping them do this.

As the Group grew bigger it was unclear who should be servicing and supporting the service user members of the Group. Service users became marginalised and occasionally found they had not been informed of important details such as cancellations of meetings etc. This is the sort of process that happens very easily in bureaucracies and needs to be deliberately counteracted.

Advantages

Suggestions made by basic grade staff and by service users were heard quickly and at a very high level in the Department. Many of the ideas were taken up and the difficulties of implementing them ironed out successfully in this Group. It was, in addition, a good opportunity for service users and workers who were often dotted all over the Borough to meet, and it provided a lot of support for the Group members.

ETHICS ADVISORY GROUP

This was a group of people comprising three workers and four people living together in the Borough affected by HIV, who came together to act as a sort of "conscience" of the Borough's system for monitoring service delivery to people affected by HIV. It was chaired by a team manager. The initial concern about the monitoring system was that service users' confidentiality might be compromised by it, though this turned out not to be the case.

Disadvantages

The monitoring system is complicated and difficult to understand. The Group members often became bedazzled by its complications.

Advantages

Because of the almost equal numbers of service users and "council officers" there was a real feeling of sharing. Some important contributions were made by the service users, which have been retained to this day. Added to this, money was available to pay expenses for the service users which was felt to be appropriate and much appreciated.

JOINT PLANNING TEAM (HIV)

I was a member of this group, which brought together people who represented the Health Authority, Social Services, voluntary organisations and local service users, for two years. Another member (a representative from the Community Health Council) and I put together a pack for the service users and voluntary organisations who took part. To a degree this was helpful, but again the service users felt marginalised by the vast quantity of informal information held by members from the Health

Authority and Social Services. The vast quantity of written and verbal information that they were given couldn't overcome this.

The other problem was that one or two of the service users involved in sub-groups that put together papers on specific issues felt that they put in an enormous amount of work on reports that seemed to "disappear", since the materials in such reports might only re-emerge six to twelve months later as part of other more extensive reports. This can be a demoralising experience for people who are not inside the organisation, and involved only in the short term, since the long term usefulness of their contributions is not obvious.

QUARTERLY INDEPENDENT SECTOR FORUM

This is a quarterly meeting held between Hammersmith and Fulham HIV Unit and all the voluntary agencies with whom the Unit has service level agreements. It provides an important opportunity for collecting feedback about service users' needs and their views.

INVOLVING SERVICE USERS AT A LOCAL LEVEL

The Quality Assurance Group has been running for over a year in Area 4 Fulham. It meets monthly and is convened by the community workers. All new service users are told about it and encouraged to join. It has the advantage of being an open and informal group, but the disadvantage of a fluid membership, although there is a committed core group. This Group is discussed in more detail in the chapter included here by Gareth Walton.

GUIDELINES FOR INVOLVING SERVICE USERS

A summary of what we learned from our experiences will help to indicate possible pitfalls:

- Only involve service users if the organisation is genuinely going to listen to them. Tokenism is all too easy. Think through first of all how you intend to involve service users in the process of a group, before inviting them to join it.

- Make sure that there is a particular worker who is specifically responsible for helping the service users. For instance, someone must make sure that they known where and when the meetings are, and if there are any cancellations they must be informed. The worker must make sure that service users can actually get to meetings, that meetings are at convenient times and venues, and that refreshments are available. These are very basic issues but easily overlooked.

- Don't make meetings top heavy with "officers".

- Be careful to use language that is easily understood - sometimes having a "translator" or mediator may be helpful. Seeing service users outside meetings is useful for building bridges and enabling genuine partnerships.

- One service user can never represent all the service users. Think about widening representation in terms of race, class, gender etc. But even though everyone is not represented it is always better to involve some service users rather than none at all.

- In terms of power, remember that most service users feel very disempowered by large organisations, and particularly by social services. Realising this is only the first step to redressing the balance of power, but often not even this step is taken. Encouraging service users to make links with voluntary organisations who can offer advice and support their involvement in statutory services can be helpful.

- Finally, remember that service providers will never set up services that service users want if those service users or potential service users are not involved in the process of defining needs and identifying the appropriate services.

Working Together (3): Changing Providers' Expectations

FRANCES HASLER

"People don't want to live in a separate state of welfare". The words are Peter Beresford's in his contribution to this volume, and the sentiments are widely shared. Disabled people are asking for independence and integration. What we too often get is enforced dependency and segregation. Changing this - creating inclusive, user-led services - takes commitment.

Service users need more than policy statements and goodwill in order to change the world. *Access* - to information, to transport, to buildings, to income - is vital. Without it we are literally shut out. *Support* - to gain confidence to ask for more, to understand the rules by which the other side is playing - is vital too. When you have been disempowered for a long time, getting your act together it tough. *Resources* - to provide those missing services, to keep us in touch with each other, to give us something to exercise choice about - are needed.

Changing the world may mean changing who we work with. In particular it may mean including black and minority ethnic people in the mainstream of what we do, not on the periphery or as an afterthought. If they have been on the margin in current services, bringing them to centre stage in user-led services needs deliberate planning, resourcing and a willingness to do things differently. This includes a willingness to give up some decision-making, perhaps some budgets, to transfer some real power.

A key to achieving the changes disabled people want is understanding the meanings of the terms "dependent" and "independent". A traditional view is that someone who needs assistance with breathing, eating and other bodily functions is a "highly dependent" person. The traditional response to this has been to arrange institutional care for such a person. The social model of disability suggests that if that same person can get assistance with their bodily functions in their own home, if they can control that assistance (perhaps by directly employing the people who provide it) then they are independent. Indeed, increasing numbers of disabled people do just this. So, the difference between dependent and independent is not about physical or mental functioning, it is about the way services are delivered and available. Services which continue to promote dependence will continue to lock people into a separate state of welfare, and will continue to create disability.

In order to create services which foster independence, service providers need to change the ways they relate to disabled people. This means confronting personal fears and prejudice as well as institutional responses. If you cannot imagine a worthwhile life for yourself as a disabled person, how does that influence the sort of life you offer to the disabled people who use your services? It is telling that service providers report more success in consulting and working with carers' groups than with disabled people's groups. Could this be because carers do not challenge the traditional view of dependency? Indeed they often refer to those they care for as "dependants".

If disabled people don't want "care", do we want what social services have to offer? Do user-led services have any role for existing workers? I think the answer has to be yes, but on new terms.

Our collective voice needs to be resourced. User-led services do not happen without users getting together to think and plan; no major service provider would work without planning, without consulting colleagues. We need to do the same. Providers have a panoply of helpers, of officers, of faxes. We need a proportion of that. We need to create user-run centres of expertise - centres of independent living. We need to ensure that they do not reproduce old inequalities. We need to be accessible from the outset to people from minority ethnic groups, people from all backgrounds and lifestyles

One of the best things service providers can do is to support our self organisation. This is not to devalue real skills - at different times in our lives disabled people need specialist help, just like everyone else. It is to say that help should not be contingent on giving up autonomy.

Working to develop user-led services is in some ways working without a map. Old definitions crumble. New ones take time to come clear. When providers talk to users, they can find that their expectations of the services are different from those that were planned for; that the value users put on the help they get is at variance with the intentions of the providers. User-led services will look different, feel different: for example a personal assistance scheme managed by disabled people compared to a traditional home help agency, or a drop-in centre managed by its users as compared to a day centre run by a local authority. Perhaps one of the biggest differences in some people's services will be the inclusion of black and minority ethnic people as service users for the first time. If they are designing the service it will be accessible to them.

The separate state of welfare has been constructed on the notion that "we" are not like "you". We are seen as dependent, needy, vulnerable. We may be all those things at some stage in our lives - so may you. It only becomes a permanent state if someone else's solution to your problem makes it so.

Part Four:

Building Models for Change

Service Evaluation by People with Learning Difficulties

ANDREA WHITTAKER, JOYCE KERSHAW AND
JOHN SPARGO

BACKGROUND

In 1989 North West Thames Regional Health
Authority began to look at ways of checking the
quality of community services for people leaving long-
stay hospitals. In discussions with officers from
Hillingdon Social Services (who had been at the
forefront of hospital resettlements in the region) it
was decided to explore a somewhat radical and
untried approach: to commission the self-advocacy
group of people with learning difficulties, People
First, to undertake an evaluation on behalf of the
Regional Health Authority. Two residential homes in
Hillingdon were chosen for evaluation, but broadly
speaking the framework and methodology were left to
People First.

It is worth commenting on the environment and
culture that formed the context of the People First
study, and indeed helped to generate this initiative in
the first place. Empowerment does not happen in a
vacuum. It evolves from a long chain of factors. In
Hillingdon these included the following significant
indicators:

- a well developed self-advocacy service;

- high consumer involvement in discussions about the principles that need to underpin policies and services;

- personal action planning to evolve unique contracts between service users and providers, established through a carefully prepared and very client-centred process;

- the active involvement of service users in helping to shape the form of major changes in services.

These are indicators of a culture in which the role of users has stepped beyond consultation to participation: real signs of an enabling organisation moving towards an empowering one.

The People First evaluation is not, therefore, a model that would either work or be acceptable in other organisations or settings unless some or all of these important and positive attitudes to the role of service users are already in place.

DESCRIPTION

The evaluation examined the lives of seven people living in two houses in Hillingdon - three in one house, four in the other. The evaluation was carried out by two members of People First, Simon Gardner and Joyce Kershaw. They were supported by Andrea Whittaker, Senior Project Officer in the Community Living Development Team at the King's Fund Centre.

Preparation for the evaluation began in February 1990 with a consultation of People First members who all had experience of living both in institutions and in the community. Information collected at this and subsequent meetings formed the basis from which questionnaires were developed. Evaluation was effected through formal interviews, informal interviews and observations. The report was handed to the Regional Health Authority in July 1990. The evaluation was itself evaluated by Libby Cooper, Director of Charities Evaluation Services.

Simon Gardner and Joyce Kershaw interviewed all the residents and spent time with them in their day centres and their leisure activities, including evening activities. They also interviewed family members and 11 staff - five working directly with the residents, two day centre managers, two hostel managers and one senior manager in charge of services. People First members devised different questionnaires for each of these different groups.

WHY THIS EVALUATION IS IMPORTANT

Valuable work has been done by researchers both here and abroad on how to make the views of service users an integral part of creating quality services. However, most of this work has been done by researchers taking the lead on methods and interviewing. As far as we are aware, this is the first time that people with learning difficulties have been given the task - with the necessary back-up resources - of undertaking an evaluation of services for their peer group. People with learning difficulties themselves drew up the questionnaires, carried out the interviews and agreed the conclusions. This evaluation put service users "in the driving seat" - calling on support and skills from other people as needed.

The evaluation was an important recognition of the

value of the opinion of people who use services and the unique contribution they can make in monitoring and evaluation. Having experienced the life of a person with a disability and having experienced receiving services, they can comment in a way which is not possible for anyone else.

CONSULTING PEOPLE FIRST MEMBERS

The evaluation process began with a consultation meeting in February 1990 with members of People First, all of whom had experience of living in a group home. Participants came up with the following list of topics which they felt were important to include in the evaluation:

- living with other people
- visitors/friends/families/neighbours
- privacy
- rotas/rules/rights
- having a job
- relating to staff
- organising leisure activities.

Several further sessions with People First members resulted in a total of 25 different topic areas being included in the questionnaires, covering all aspects of a person's life.

INTERVIEWING

Simon and Joyce shared the interviewing. Sometimes they were both involved in interviewing one person: sometimes one or other did an interview on their own. Joyce developed considerable skill in using the questionnaires to record information. Simon did not do any writing, but was particularly skilled in asking relevant supplementary questions. Andrea sat in on all interviews except one and also filled in a questionnaire.

Joyce and Simon became adept at explaining questions to people when necessary - perhaps when the question was too abstract or the person didn't seem to understand what was being asked. Sometimes they "acted out" an example to help make it clearer. Both consultants recorded additional impressions and opinions outside the interview situation - Joyce writing notes and Simon using a dictaphone.

RESULTS

For detailed results on each aspect of the residents' lives, readers need to consult the full report (Whittaker, Gardner and Kershaw, 1991). Here we give only a brief summary based on the way we summarised results in the report. We adapted a way of looking at people's lives which was developed by John O'Brien, an American who works for better lives for people with learning difficulties (O'Brien, 1986). He identified five areas of people's lives which should be looked at when judging quality of life:

- community presence
- relationships
- choice
- competence
- respect.

The consultants looked at all five aspects when thinking about the people in the two houses. In the end, it was decided to leave out the last area - respect - because during the two weeks at the houses there were not enough opportunities to observe people interacting with ordinary members of the public to make a significant judgement.

Community presence

- **The houses:** both houses scored well. The residents live in houses which are like other homes around them and are in an ordinary street. In their new homes, the residents are "in the community".

- Daytime living (working hours): in the first house, one person had a full-time job, so was "in the community", but the other two people went to the day centre five days a week. The second house scored 50/50 on this. Although two people still went to a day centre, the other two had been spending their daytime hours mostly away from social services settings. Of these, one was soon going to college full-time and steps had been taken to help the fourth man to get a job.

- Leisure: neither house scored well. All the residents still relied on leisure activities which were linked to services. Residents did go to the pub - but that was with a member of staff.

Relationships

Neither house scored well. Most of the people the residents came into contact with, apart from their families, were other people with disabilities or people paid to be with them. Many of the staff were very aware of this and were really trying to work out ways to change this situation.

Choice

All the residents had lots of small choices in their

lives, mainly within their own homes, for example choosing clothes, food, bedtimes. They had very few large choices, for example, alternatives to going to a day centre. Residents at one house had more choice about what to do in their spare time, even though most of the choices were within services.

Competence
Again, in their own homes, all the residents were getting help to learn new skills. But neither house scored well in the areas of daytime activities or leisure.

The two areas where we learned the most about what needs to be improved in the future were in the time needed to prepare for the work, and the need to be more skilled in communicating with people who don't use words. The information we had before we began the evaluation did not prepare us for the severity of these communication problems. Two residents in particular presented us with challenges which we could not adequately overcome.

For example, one young man was just beginning to learn letters, words and numbers using picture cards, and his spoken vocabulary was very limited. Simon recorded his experience of interviewing this young man:

> "I felt physically and mentally drained from this interview, because I haven't got the skills to sign in Makaton. I had to make the questions a little bit simpler so that I could make Paul understand what I was trying to ask him. I had to show him one thing - it was about privacy - like if someone was in the bathroom, having a bath or was on

---

What worked well/what could have been better in the evaluation

The following is a summary:

Worked well	Could have been better
We worked well together as a team	Parts of questionnaires: • difficult questions • abstract questions
Recording the information	We needed more time to get to know people in the houses before we interviewed them
Helping people understand the questions	More preparation time needed eg. to draw up questionnaires, to work out different ways of interviewing
Practical organisation: • support at King's Fund Centre • support at Hillingdon	Number of interviews with distant family members requiring travelling: • driving • not knowing the area

We all enjoyed it!

---

the loo, about knocking on the door when a resident was in there. I think he understood that question after I had physically showed him what I meant, rather than explaining it to him.

"Half way through the interview, Joyce took over because I was beginning to feel shattered and Joyce finished the interview. When she had finished, she looked shattered as well."

The actual two weeks for doing the visits and interviews, although tiring, worked well on the whole. Drawing up the timetable, which in the end involved 19 interviews and ten visits, was complicated but not impossible, thanks to the willing co-operation of the staff and residents of both houses. It would have been better to have allowed more time to prepare for the work - to develop the questionnaires and learn more about interviewing.

There should have been a longer gap between when we first met the residents and when the interviews started. We would have then had more chance to seek advice and work out the best way of interviewing people, particularly those who used signing to communicate. In order to get to know one of the residents in particular, we would have had to spend a lot more time than was available in this evaluation.

Two Years On

In many ways, the evaluation and report became swept up in the surge of energy and change that the National Health Service and Community Care Act has created. Most if not all of the practical steps recommended in the evaluation have been taken, and the world and lives of the people directly involved in the study have moved on, as one would expect. But the model of the evaluation and its positive and successful outcome has given Hillingdon a range of insights which have been built into the thinking about service inspection and standard setting, and the way in which service users can and should be involved in a very central way to these processes.

Actual examples include:

- a user/carer forum planning the future shape and form of daytime services;

- user groups working alongside inspectors in the arms-length inspection of residential homes;

- a user group working alongside officers to look at the way respite services are provided.

As with the People First evaluation, each of these examples has required a radical re-think of the way we look at services, the language and jargon we often use, and of how inaccessible many traditional planning approaches are to people who use services. But major strides have been made in the past 12 to 18 months in improving the role of service users in planning and decision making, and currently attention is being given to ways in which service users can influence the joint commissioning of services which have been established as part of the implementation of the Act.

The People First evaluation led the way in challenging traditional models, stereotypes and assumptions. It applied a refreshingly human and outcome-led philosophy to the business of looking at quality and has given us a very clear reminder that our services are about people with very strong views about what they like and do not like, and that by ignoring the crucial information within these personal views and opinions, we ignore a way to develop services which properly meet the needs and wishes of the individuals for whom they are intended.

KEY ELEMENTS FOR SUCCESS IN A USER-LED EVALUATION

All three members of the evaluation team learnt a lot from doing this work. What follows is a summary of what we feel are the most important points to consider in undertaking similar work.

Commitment from service managers

Securing commitment from people at all levels in the service to be evaluated is the vital first stage in any work of this nature. Words are not enough. They must be backed up with resources, support, and a commitment to take action on the findings.

This evaluation would not have happened without the commitment and enthusiasm of key senior managers in Hillingdon Social Services Department and North West Thames Regional Health Authority. These people were prepared not only to work together across service boundaries to reach agreement in principle to such a new undertaking, but to back this up with appropriate financial and other resources - for example fees, expenses, office accommodation.

Commitment from "grassroots" staff

The fact that Hillingdon had a well-established policy of involving service users, demonstrated in practice, meant that staff supporting people in their day-to-day lives welcomed this initiative and were ready and willing to co-operate with the evaluators.

Involve service users right from the start

It is crucial to involve people with learning difficulties at every stage. This is a basic principle underpinning this work, since it is important to make sure that the "ownership" of the work remains with the service users.

Provide the right support

- Personal/advisory support: it is essential that anyone providing support to service users who are involved in evaluations should be experienced in enabling people to express their own views. The supporter needs to work in such a way as to ensure that his or her views do not intrude - that the possibility of him/her influencing the service users is minimised as much as possible. The supporter needs skills in giving "neutral advice". For example, being able to suggest various options for asking questions, leaving the choice to the consultants.

- Practical support: transport, meals, accommodation, secretarial back-up, "office space" - a place that the evaluation team can call their own, for storage, for reviewing progress, for recording impressions and results, for quiet thinking and relaxing.

Allow plenty of preparation time

The amount of preparation time needs to be planned carefully. With hindsight we needed more preparation time, though we became aware also that a balance needs to be struck between allowing enough time to prepare properly and not spending so much time preparing that it spoils the initial enthusiasm and dedication to the work.

Preparation time is needed:

- to devise questionnaires allowing enough time to prepare first drafts, to get some help from a questionnaire "expert" and finally to revise them;

- to prepare the consultant and their supporter;

- to get to know the people with learning difficulties you will be interviewing.

This last point was the area where we most needed to allow more time. Although we had a profile of each person - their weekly activities, what they did in the daytime, what they did in the evenings, what they usually did at the week-end - and a certain amount of information about their ability to communicate, this was not sufficient to prepare us for some of the difficulties we encountered with people whose ability to communicate verbally was very limited.

So time must be allowed for considering carefully what will be the best way of communicating with each person. Would pictures or drawings be helpful? Do you need to take photographs of "before" and "after" situations and places? Will you need assistance with interpreting people's answers? For example, someone who is experienced at signing? It would be best if this help is provided by an outside (independent) person. Have you got the money to pay this person?

Training for the consultants

It is likely that people with learning difficulties who are going to be involved in evaluating will already have some of the necessary skills (for example experience at speaking up for themselves, the ability to get on well with people because they are interested in other people and what they think and feel). But they will need additional skills particularly relevant for evaluation. They need to learn interviewing skills. They need to work out which method of recording information will suit them best: for example writing, using a dictaphone, having someone else write their comments for them.

Teamwork

It is important that the service user consultants and their supporter work well as a team. Doing this work can be physically and emotionally tiring, and if they don't get on well, it is unlikely they will do a successful piece of work.

ISSUES FOR THE FUTURE

This evaluation is an extremely important "first" because it took the involvement of people with learning difficulties in assessing the quality of services further than it has ever gone before. Now we need to consider how we can learn from the experience in Hillingdon in order to strengthen this involvement. How does this evaluation fit in with the range of initiatives aimed at achieving and maintaining high quality services which reflect the needs and wishes of people who use those services? The following are a number of questions which we feel need to be explored further in order to develop this work in a positive way.

Involving professionals

One of the important issues for consideration for the future is how much professional expertise should be included. In the case of this evaluation, it is true that more professional involvement, at the design stage of the questionnaires for example, would have resulted in fewer inappropriate questions from a researcher's point of view, but how much of the freshness and enthusiasm of People First's ideas might have been lost - or at least "watered down" - in the process?

Perhaps, at least on this pioneering occasion, it was a good thing that the balance of input weighed heavily on People First's side.

Training for consultants

We need to build in time and resources to enable consultants to have relevant training, in interviewing techniques for example - asking supplementary questions, when to keep probing for an answer and when to stop, avoiding leading questions.

On the other hand, we do not want to turn people into quasi-researchers. Given the long history of services casting people with disabilities in a patient/pupil role, it would be all too easy to try to turn people into role models which would be acceptable to professionals but which could blunt the uniqueness of their personal contribution. How do we get the balance right?

Making a balanced judgement

In this work, we are asking for the service users' point of view, but how much can/should we help people to take into account a broader range of views and information before making a judgement? To what extent might the lack of this skill weaken the validity of the judgement? Are there certain areas where this might be important and others where it is less important?

Involving users in service evaluation at the senior level as well as grass roots level

As Libby Cooper pointed out in her evaluation of the work, the parts which proved most successful in terms of the quality of the questionnaires, the interviews and observations, and the judgements made, were those which related to people's everyday lives - home, work, day centre, leisure - and this is perhaps to be expected because it is based on service users' direct experience. The part of the evaluation, which from a researcher's point of view was less successful, was that involving staff, particularly middle and senior staff.

In developing the questionnaires for staff, People First members had very clear ideas about what they wanted to ask. For example, they were conscious of the need for staff to be properly supported; they wanted to ask questions relating to people from minority groups; they wanted to know how much service users were involved in interviewing and appointing staff. On more than one occasion, their questions took managers by surprise and made them think afresh.

To the extent that the questionnaires to managers and staff were made up of the questions which People First members wanted to ask, they achieved their purpose. The consultants were able to use the information gained to supplement their knowledge of the residents' lives and to help make judgements about the services in general. They gave a service users' view of the staff and management.

Undoubtedly service users have shown that they can contribute to the monitoring and evaluation of services at the management level as well as at "grassroots" level. For the future, we need to consider how that contribution can be strengthened.

Keeping "ownership" with the service users
However we tackle these issues in the future, we

must make sure that the support is given in partnership with service users in a way which enhances and does not supplant the unique contribution which they can make because of their own life experience.

This evaluation has shown that people with learning difficulties can take part in the monitoring and evaluation of services in a very direct way. Now there is a base line from which to explore how to develop and strengthen their involvement in such work in the future.

Building Change and Making It Stick: A Local Authority Wide Perspective

MARIAN BARNES

THE BIRMINGHAM COMMUNITY CARE SPECIAL ACTION PROJECT

Birmingham City Council started to think about how to develop community care services before the government-commissioned Griffiths Report, which led eventually to the National Health Service and Community Care Act, was published. Officers and politicians in the city were aware that, as more people were moving out of long stay psychiatric hospitals and hospitals for people with learning difficulties, and as more people were living into very old age, there were simply not enough community care resources to meet their needs.

The response was to launch an ambitious initiative designed to ensure that the best use was made of the resources of the whole City, in order to enable disabled and elderly people to live ordinary lives within the community. The two key principles guiding what became the Community Care Special Action Project (the Project) were:

- that responsibilities for community care should rest not only with Health Authorities and the Social Services Department, but with the Local Authority as a whole;

- that people who use services should be consulted, and should influence the way in which services were developed.

Whilst the scope of the Project was ambitious - it was charged with developing and co-ordinating policies across a Local Authority which serves a population of one million, and in which there were five different Health Authorities - the size of the Project team (four people) charged with this task was modest. This team had certain important characteristics:

- It was based in the City's Social Services Department, but operated at arms length from mainstream management structures and was able to work across agency boundaries and hierarchies.

- The Director of the Project team was appointed from outside the Authority. She provided charismatic leadership internally, and a high national profile for the project. Her appointment was linked with the Policy Studies Institute in London in order to increase the opportunity for national networking.

- The team reported to the Community Care Chief Officers Group which comprised all the chief officers of the Local Authority and the district general managers of the Birmingham Health Authorities.

- It was established as a time limited initiative - from January 1987 to March 1990 - with the intention that it should impact on mainstream services, rather than set up separate "projects" in parallel to the mainstream. The overall purpose was described as achieving lasting change in the organisational culture of agencies providing community care services.

EVALUATING THE PROJECT

An independent evaluation of the Project was funded by the Department of Health. It was thought to be important to learn from the experience of an initiative designed not only to enable users to have their voices heard in the development of community care services, but also one which recognised that the needs of people who use services are not determined by the organisational boundaries which serve to define and limit the responsibilities of service providers.

The evaluation was also seen as a way of encouraging change to take place through this learning process. It has aimed to reflect the values of the Project in terms of enabling users to have their voices heard in the evaluation itself. It has also aimed to set up systems which would make it possible for those voices to be heard after the evaluation was complete. My colleague Gerald Wistow and I have written about how we have tried to do this elsewhere (Barnes, 1993; Barnes and Wistow, 1992).

WHAT DID THE PROJECT DO?

The Project's work was wide ranging and it is only possible to list very briefly the main ways in which it sought to carry out its task:

- It commissioned consumer research to seek the views of users of mental health services and of disabled people about the services they were receiving or had received in the past.

- It established a pilot citizen advocacy project for people in a long stay psychiatric hospital which was due for closure.

- It supported the development of users councils for users of mental health services, both in psychiatric hospitals and in community based psychiatric services.

- It initiated a continuing series of public consultations for people who care for an elderly or disabled relative or friend.

- It held one-off public consultations for people with physical impairments and, separately, for people with sensory impairments.

- It held small scale consultations with people with learning disabilities and, separately, with carers, as part of a review of daytime opportunities for people with learning disabilities.

- Since a fundamental requirement of involvement is the improvement of the information available to people who use services, the Project pursued a variety of activities designed to help people find out more about services, and about their rights to them.

None of these activities is unique. A key factor in making the Birmingham Project "special" was the fact that they were all part of an overall programme which was intended to achieve change in the underlying culture. One of the ways in which the experience in Birmingham can help us learn is in how to develop an overall strategy for achieving user-led services. We need to understand how user input at one point within the service system needs to be supported by other types of input elsewhere.

ENABLING USERS TO BE INFLUENTIAL

The key means by which the Project aimed to enable users to exert influence was by giving them a voice. And the key purpose was seen to be to produce services which were more sensitive to users' needs. So the mechanisms and structures that were put in place were intended both to enable service users and their carers to have their say, and to ensure that change came about as a result.

Voices were heard in a number of different ways. In the case of consumer research the voices were heard indirectly through the medium of research reports. In one instance this led to opposition from the Birmingham Disability Rights Group. They felt that it would have been better if disabled people had been asked to undertake their own research, rather than bringing in non-disabled "experts" to do this. On the other hand, the research exploring the experiences of people who were users of mental health services was welcomed publicly by a young man who attended a day centre, and who was involved in presenting the findings to service providers. However, in neither case was an effective mechanism put in place for ensuring that action was taken in response to research findings. But there were other ways in which users of mental health services had their voices heard.

In the users councils, people in wards of psychiatric hospitals and in community based mental health services were enabled to develop their voices through meeting with each other and being supported in that. By getting together people can feel stronger and more confident about having their say. They may be more willing to be critical whilst talking amongst themselves than they would be in responding individually to a research interviewer. But the users councils' support worker, himself a user of services, then had a big responsibility in communicating what people had been saying to service providers. Because it was felt important that service providers should not control what happened in the users councils, there was some difficulty in ensuring that what was said in the councils influenced the way in which some service providers behaved and the decisions they reached.

As the Project was coming to an end a review of mental health services was starting to get underway. This had always been on the Project's agenda, but was only completed after it had finished. Users were involved in the steering group for this review and so were able to influence its content. Their voices were heard as members of a joint working group with responsibility for reaching decisions about what should be looked at, as well as giving their views about what needed to be changed. Building in users' voices at this planning stage is one way of ensuring that they will not be ignored.

In consultations the voices were heard directly by those hosting the meetings. In the case of the carers consultations, which had the highest profile of any of the Project's initiatives, carers' voices were heard directly by senior and chief officers who chaired the meetings, and who claimed to have been personally influenced as a result. This led to commitment to action in response to issues raised. A corporate group of senior officers - the Performance Review Group - was established with responsibility to ensure action was taken in response to 11 "action points" identified from what people had to say at the consultations. This group allocated responsibility for the 11 issues to different chief officers within the City and asked for progress reports to monitor what was happening. As part of the research evaluation of the Project, two panels of carers were also actively involved in monitoring progress on these issues.

The consultations with people with learning disabilities undertaken as part of the service review enabled a small number of users - 13 - to have their voices heard. However, the outcome of the review was more important in terms of trying to ensure that users were able to influence both their individual care plans, and the way in which daytime opportunities for people with learning disabilities were developed more generally. A "service development initiative" was launched in one part of the city. This was carried out through existing service management structures and included a commitment to the development of "shared individual programme plans"; to supporting user groups within day centres; and to developing individualised opportunities for people through the work of community placements officers.

Thus the Birmingham Project provides different examples of ways of hearing voices, and different models of trying to achieve change as a result.

OUTCOMES

What have been the outcomes and achievements deriving from this work?

Commitment to improving existing services

Most of the issues identified through consultations with carers were about improving the quality and quantity of existing services, rather than about radical change in the nature of services. The City publicly committed itself to making such improvements.

It takes a long time to make changes to services and many of the carers involved in the panels have expressed considerable scepticism about the extent to which real change has occurred. But it is possible to point to some specific developments, for example, the development of the Birmingham Information File to improve basic information about community care services provided by all agencies and to enable people to access services they didn't know existed, and the installation of a helpline to enable carers to call for help out of normal office hours. The action point agenda is still alive, albeit reduced and in a somewhat different form.

New service models

Consultations with disabled people and with people with learning disabilities identified the need for new types of service which would enable people to move towards work, rather than remain as attenders of segregated day centres. Whilst the somewhat ambitious aim of getting 100 disabled people into jobs within a year has not been met, there are a number of ways in which services have changed to achieve the aim of enabling more people to work: day centres are making links with colleges to develop training courses; community placement officers are seeking individual work opportunities for the people they work with; and a new unit - "Employability" - has been established in the City's Economic Development Department with a remit to work with both employers and service providers to develop work opportunities for disabled people.

New definitions of "problems"

People who use services often define their problems differently from those who provide services. Accepting that day services should be designed to move people towards employment, rather than to provide lifelong daytime occupation, indicated a move away from seeing community care as welfare.

Another important "problem" related to mobility. Disabled people clearly identify this as a problem of the environment, rather than a problem which is located in *them*. Another outcome of the Project's work has been the establishment of a "Mobility Task Group" with a remit to bring about change both in transport services and in the physical environment of the City to ensure that people are not excluded from ordinary activities because they cannot get to them. This Group demonstrates how redefining the problem means that responsibility for action has to involve people not usually thought to have responsibility for "community care". Members of the Task Group include architects and engineers, as well as people from Social Services and from the City's Central Policy Unit. The Group also includes a disabled woman and the mother of a disabled person.

DEVELOPING USER INVOLVEMENT

One of the basic lessons to be learnt has been that "user involvement" cannot be a one-off activity if real change is to be achieved. In a variety of ways users and carers have continued to have their voices heard after the Project has formally come to an end. In addition to the means mentioned above, users and carers have been involved in a "Search Team" established to maintain the impetus of the project; a carer has been a member of the Performance Review Group; there has been wide consultation in relation to the implementation of the National Health Service and Community Care Act; and a project called "Learning from Service Users" was established to broaden the lessons to all Council services, not just those concerned with community care.

SOME IMPLICATIONS OF THE PROJECT'S APPROACH

The Project adopted a broad approach to achieving change through the involvement of service users. It operated "top-down" to the extent that it was established as a result of a decision taken at the top of the Local Authority and it aimed to generate commitment at the most senior level in order to ensure that change would be supported throughout the Authority. What are the consequences of this approach?

- Taking a City-wide perspective has ensured that responsibility for community care is accepted by departments other than Social Services. This has proved important in moving away from a definition of community care as welfare, to one which is capable of responding to people's wishes to live ordinary lives.

- It is very difficult to sustain and develop consistent change across such a broad spectrum. Some issues have dropped by the wayside as the Project moved to the detailed implementation phase.

- Some voices are heard more loudly than others. Certainly in terms of numbers, more carers than direct service users have been heard. The carers consultations were also uppermost in the minds of officers interviewed as part of the evaluation. This affects both the change agenda identified, and what might be considered effective models of involvement.

- The emphasis has been on collective models of involvement designed to influence service managers. There is also a need to change the behaviour of front-line providers - doctors, community nurses, social workers, and day centre workers - so that their practice enables participation in decision-making at an individual level. The Project did not provide models for participative practice between providers and users. Collective consultation cannot be an alternative for partnership between providers and users in their day to day encounters. Partnership at this individual level is also important to ensure that the majority voices which may be heard in collective discussions do not determine the change agenda for minorities who may have different interests and needs.

- Because of the high profile achieved by the Project and the public commitment of senior people within the Authority, there has been a commitment to continue and develop means of involving users and carers. Whilst the initiatives developed during the lifetime of the project had various degrees of success in the short term, there is a general acceptance that service development should continue to be influenced by the views of users and the groundwork has been laid for determining how this can happen most effectively in different contexts.

Finally, returning to my perspective on this as a researcher, I think research has an important part to play in helping people learn from experiences such as that of the Birmingham Community Care Special Action Project. Through research we can learn what different groups want and expect from being involved, and what outcomes can be achieved, both in terms of service changes and in the personal impacts on those involved. These can be considered the "findings" of research. But research also has a role and a responsibility in developing means by which people can be involved in the research process itself. This poses challenges for researchers which are similar to those facing service providers. We all have much to learn about changing relationships between those who provide and those who receive services and that requires an openness to learning on the part of all involved in that process.

NOTE

I am grateful to the Department of Health for funding the research on which this article is based. The views expressed do not necessarily represent the view of the Department.

Self-Advocacy by Black People with Learning Difficulties

JACKIE DOWNER AND PETER FERNS

BLACK DISABLED PEOPLE IN SOCIETY

In this discussion "Black" is used as a political term, to stand for solidarity or togetherness for people who experience racism because of their skin colour. By using the term "Black" it is hoped to give people support and confidence to stand up against racism and not feel alone. It is spelled here with a capital letter to remind us that it is a political term and not just a description of skin colour.

The experience of Black people with learning difficulties is part of the wider experience of Black disabled people in society. Black disabled people have been subjected to a particular form of oppression: a combination of racism and disablism. They are seen in a racist way as aggressive, dangerous, a burden, lazy, less able than they really are, condemned as criminals and more likely to be labelled as schizophrenics. Thinking of groups of Black people in such negative and insulting ways is racist stereotyping and does not give people respect as individuals.

Nor are Black disabled people given chances to have more power over their own lives, to feel confident enough to fight against the discrimination that they face everyday. "Care services" and many of the professionals who work in them are not aware how often Black disabled people have power taken away from them, often by the services themselves. Few services are really suited to the needs of Black disabled people, respect their cultural backgrounds or make them feel strong and confident as Black people.

There are hardly any positive images or role models to give Black disabled people inspiration or a sense of pride. More often they are seen as even more "pitiful" than white disabled people or more "tragic" because of poverty in a "developing" country. Given such discrimination and such attitudes towards Black disabled people, it is not surprising that Black people with learning difficulties are seen as child-like, pathetic and in need of "care"; or as threatening, aggressive and in need of "control".

In this discussion we will put forward some reasons why self-advocacy is particularly important for Black people with learning difficulties, and examine how it can lead to greater "personal empowerment": that is, having more power and control over your own life. The ideas discussed here come from self-advocacy groups of Black people with learning difficulties in which the authors have been involved.

COMMON EXPERIENCES

The most common experiences for Black people with learning difficulties are:

- having your culture disregarded
- being ignored as a Black person
- being treated as if you were a white person
- being called racist names

- not having your religious beliefs taken seriously
- feeling alone, particularly in hospitals and hostels
- having your confidence taken away
- being given a thousand excuses why you cannot do things
- not being listened to
- being told what to do all the time by staff and families
- having to fight hard to be seen as a strong black person
- having to fight hard for equal respect with others.

WHAT IS SELF-ADVOCACY?

Self-advocacy can help to reduce negative experiences and increase positive experiences for Black people with learning difficulties. We asked members of Black advocacy groups to tell us what speaking up for themselves meant. They came up with the following answers :

- thinking for yourself
- saying what you think
- having relationships like anyone else
- people listening to you
- making mistakes
- taking risks
- changing people's racist views about yourself
- taking responsibility for yourself
- making decisions
- feeling good about yourself
- feeling good about your own culture and way of life
- standing up for your rights
- getting respect for who you are, as a Black person with learning difficulties.

WHY SELF-ADVOCACY?

Making sure people listen to you and know what you want is very important for people who have little power and are likely be treated unfairly. There are lots of different ways of getting your views and interests across to workers and professionals in care services but speaking for yourself is by far the best. People are likely to be much more confident about their own abilities and have greater control over their own lives if they are enabled to speak for themselves.

Self-advocacy helps all people to know what they really want and be stronger in standing up for their rights. It further helps Black people with learning difficulties to be proud to be Black and disabled, and challenge the negative images in the newspapers and on television. Black people with learning difficulties often need their own space before they feel confident about being on equal terms even with non-disabled Black people.

People in power in care services, usually white people, have to listen to Black service users to provide suitable services in terms of culture, food, dress, ways of life, religions etc. Black people should have respect for their own culture and be helped to deal with racism. One very important source of support for Black service users is their own families. Services should support Black families and help Black communities understand the needs of disabled people. Black people with learning difficulties must also deal with lack of understanding and prejudices about disability within Black communities and sometimes their own families. This is not to suggest that people might want to leave their families or weaken their ties, but that they may need help in getting their own interests across. Many Black parents and carers themselves need support because of their own experiences of racism in services.

What Is a Self-Advocacy Group?

A self-advocacy group has to :

- be independent of services and workers;

- have funding without any "strings" attached;

- be controlled by people with learning difficulties;

- be advised by experienced disabled people and/or non-disabled people skilled in enabling self-advocacy;

- not be shaped by the "outside" expectations of non-disabled people;

- be given space and time to grow and develop;

- be built on the strengths of the group members;

- be taken seriously by services which should not pretend to support self-advocacy when they really do not;

- have their advice and decisions listened to carefully and acted upon by service workers;

- have real power and representation in important decisions about the service which affect users' lives;

- become a pressure group for positive change in services;

- empower group members to change their own lives with the support of other disabled people.

BARRIERS TO BLACK SELF-ADVOCACY

The main barrier to self-advocacy by Black people with learning difficulties is that other people often do not really want to listen. There is a lot of "tokenism" or pretending to listen to disabled people, whether they are Black or white, but racial prejudice can result in discrimination even within the self-advocacy movement itself. For example, very few Black people are actively involved and representation in self-advocacy groups is poor. The racist view is that Black disabled people do not have anything positive to say, and Black people with learning difficulties are especially likely to be seen as child-like and not very responsible.

Another major barrier is the threat felt by workers and professionals in care services when service users start to make demands and challenge their power and authority. If the group making the challenge is Black, this increases their feelings of being threatened. The lack of Black workers and professionals with real influence makes such challenges less effective since those in power are usually white, non-disabled people. Awareness must be raised generally about self-advocacy and its importance for good quality services, and within Black communities especially.

DIFFICULTIES AND BENEFITS IN SETTING UP A BLACK SELF-ADVOCACY GROUP

We have found that transport and getting around the community are big problems for many group members. Transport is often hard to arrange or arrives late. Sometimes staff from a residential or day care establishment would drive a minibus or car, but only if enough staff were on duty. Often group members who could come on their own were either not allowed to or lacked the confidence. Finding the best time to meet could be difficult if some people preferred to meet during the day and others in the early evening. We held most of our meetings in the evenings, but have also been involved with daytime groups.

Whatever time is agreed, for people living in residential establishments the attitudes of staff are very important and can decide whether people attend or not. We have practised dealing with staff who are reluctant to bring people to meetings because they are busy or do not see them as important. We have found that staff feel threatened by the meetings because they do not know what goes on and cannot see any "results" in their terms. White staff in particular and white service users are also often uneasy about Black people meeting together because it reminds them that racism is still a problem for Black people.

The meetings themselves can be difficult, because group members are not used to speaking out and saying what they feel. People who are used to being told what to do find it hard doing things for themselves and are afraid of making mistakes until they see that this is a way of learning. It takes time for them to overcome these difficulties and feel comfortable in the group.

The benefits are that people become excited and interested, find it easier to talk and become more confident about themselves and their opinions. They feel more important and feel good about being Black, because they have stood up for themselves and made decisions for themselves, and because they have found out more about what other Black people are doing in this country. There has also been a lot of interest in the groups in Black history and the cultures of different countries.

SERVICE SUPPORT FOR SELF-ADVOCACY GROUPS

To actively support self-advocacy for service users, services and service workers should follow these guidelines:

- Make a public commitment to support self-advocacy and to recognise that it is an important way of empowering users.

- Take positive steps to make sure that self-advocacy happens in residential and day care establishments.

- Inform Black communities about the value of self-advocacy for disabled people.

- Set up systems for talking to self-advocacy groups and take their views seriously.

- Support and encourage Black disabled people to be part of service planning.

- Get resources to support and develop self-advocacy.

- Make sure that self-advocacy is put into practice in all areas of daily living.

- Help people set up self-advocacy groups without taking them over and making them part of services.

- Find Black advisers to self-advocacy groups who are not part of the local services and are as independent as possible.

- Make sure that self-advocates are given real power in decision-making in services.

- Give Black disabled people time and space to meet as self-advocates.

- Provide people with the necessary assistance to attend self-advocacy groups, such as transport.

- If a person wishes to attend a self-advocacy group, look on this as very important.

- Train Black and white staff and managers about self-advocacy, and provide training for white users about race issues.

- Train workers to develop skills to help disabled people take more part in everyday living tasks, choices and decisions.

- Help Black disabled people to be more involved in training staff.

Empowering Disabled People in Assessment: Positive Initiatives

KATHRYN ELLIS

A RESEARCH STUDY

This discussion is based on the findings of a two and a half year research project funded by the Joseph Rowntree Foundation to look at the assessment practice of social services departments in relation to people with disabilities and their informal carers (Ellis, 1993). The research aimed to explore:

- how far service users and their carers were involved in assessments and how much choice and control they had over their life-styles as a result;

- what the significance of the findings was for full implementation of the National Health Service and Community Care Act in April 1993 when social services departments take a lead role in the assessment of people with disabilities and their carers for community care services.

The fieldwork was carried out in two local authorities between October 1990 and June 1991, by a mix of:

- observing assessments carried out by a range of practitioners, notably occupational therapists, social workers, home care managers;

- interviewing users, carers and practitioners about particular assessments;

- interviewing managers and groups of practitioners about assessment practice;

- analysing documentation such as policy and operational manuals and information leaflets provided to users and carers.

THE FINDINGS

In discussing assessment with practitioners and observing their practice, the following broad conclusions were reached:

- *Professionalism*: many professional assessors had a sense of expertise which limited the amount of information they shared with the people they were assessing and the opportunity they gave them to raise issues for themselves, because as practitioners they tended to assume they knew better than users and carers what their priorities should be.

- *Practice wisdom*: because practitioners regarded assessment as a task they could carry out without conscious effort, they tended to rely on their practice experience to make decisions about people's needs. But informal judgements could be as oppressive as professional expertise, particularly as they would rarely be shared with the people being assessed. Assumptions would be made about caring situations in different cultures for example, or about the giving and receiving of care by people from all ethnic backgrounds. And practice wisdom frequently incorporated moral judgements about how self-reliant people were - or how clean and tidy!

- *Assessment as rationing*: assessment is not just a means of identifying people's needs but of allocating scarce resources to meet those needs. Assessors would limit the amount of time they spent with users and carers, control what happened during that time and offer stereotyped responses to situations based on the resources with which they were familiar and to which they had ready access. Again, the techniques assessors developed to manage the resources at their disposal were not shared so that any opportunity people had to influence the outcome was considerably reduced.

So far as users and carers were concerned, the following broad conclusions were reached on the basis of separate discussions with them about their expectations and experience of social services:

- *Primacy of informal support*: the majority of people with disabilities turned first to their informal network for practical and emotional support. People with disabilities would often limit their demands on both formal and informal carers through a preference for remaining self-reliant, whilst users and carers sought to preserve their privacy and the integrity of carefully orchestrated caring routines by not introducing services.

- *Formal / informal care:* the choices people were enabled to make about their preferred lifestyles were limited by the capacity of providers to respond appropriately to caring situations. As noted above, assessors would make oppressive assumptions about such situations, notably the giving of personal care by close partners, and options were further limited by the rationing of services and practitioners' time.

- *Negotiating power*: people's ability to make demands was further limited by language and cultural barriers and by the unavailability of appropriate information at the right time. And because so many of the judgements and decisions of assessors were not made explicit, those being assessed had difficulty challenging them. Strategies such as getting angry or threatening to withdraw informal support were often effective but only at a cost, in terms of the distress they caused to users and carers.

SIGNIFICANCE FOR POLICY AND PRACTICE

Guidance to social services department managers and practitioners by the Social Services Inspectorate on implementing the National Health Service and Community Care Act emphasises the cultural shift which will be required to move current assessment practice in the direction of greater user and carer participation. This research study has shown that the effect of the ways practitioners think about need is very often to obscure or exclude users' and carers' assessments of their own priorities.

But the fact that assessors perform the dual, often conflicting function of identifying need and determining eligibility produces the most damaging behaviour, both in terms of failing to involve the people being assessed in the process and limiting the options made available. Because practitioners are placed in the position of managing too many demands with too few resources they develop strategies to control those demands which are largely informal, implicit and so unavailable for challenge by those being assessed. All these influences are reinforced by the way users and carers limit their own demands on services and the difficulty they have in taking on service providers.

Unless tackling the values and attitudes deeply embedded in assessment practice is taken as a priority issue by service providers, the danger will be that the process of assessment becomes divorced from its wider organisational and political context. The temptation for service providers will be to focus on developing more tangible products of change such as assessment criteria and pro-formas but all the while discounting their accountability to users and carers by failing to advocate on their behalf.

Positive initiatives for change must therefore emphasise the following:

- *Broadening definitions of need:* in order for individual users and carers to be able to exercise choice in assessment, organisations of disabled people and carers should be separately involved in setting the agenda for service provision - through contracting arrangements, for example. Further "unmet need" should be thought of not just in terms of service deficits but in terms of local discriminatory structures and practices, so that community care acquires a meaning closer to the real priorities of people with disabilities and their informal carers.

- *Empowering users and carers*: people being assessed need clear, timely and relevant information about organisational priorities and options for support available locally, as well as access to independent advocacy in order to make demands on services and, where necessary, challenge decisions made by providers. People can also be empowered by the opportunity to come together with others sharing common experiences, including that of oppression.

- *Assessment as negotiation:* providing training for practitioners which changes the language of assessment from that of "meeting need" to that of negotiation and compromise between user, carer and provider, and helps them acknowledge the differing priorities and power people bring to assessment. Equalising power between the participants also means ensuring the process of rationing is made explicit so all concerned are fully aware of the rules of the game before a negotiated settlement is reached.

Working Together (4): Who Do *You* Represent...?

DAVID KEAY

"But you're not like *my* clients..." If I had a crisp tenner every time that "argument" was used to counter my entire presentation on increasing the involvement or participation of people who use mental health services in the planning and provision of services, I would probably be better paid than those who level the charge. "Who do *you* represent..." That's my other favourite. A similar financial deal on that one and I'd be in the league of an National Health Service Trust director!

I enjoy a well reasoned argument. I admire the professional who can construct a defence of their service, or who can constructively criticise my ideas. I am open-minded enough to learn from such exchanges. The type of professional who argues in this way will usually benefit from the discussion. But why is so much valuable time and energy wasted on what is little more than a personal attack, the first defence of a frightened traditionalist who hasn't bothered to listen to a word of the twenty minute presentation that invariably precedes the charges?

"But you're not like *my* clients..." : the "articulate user" syndrome. The first difference between me and his - for it is invariably a man - clients is that I have a platform, an opportunity to have my say, a genuine prospect of being heard. He is the type of professional who sees the professional/client roles as rigidly defined. I have been treated by professionals of that type. He is not interested in what his client has to say anyway.

His clients are probably disempowered by months or years of not being listened to. Then they are disempowered by being asked to get involved, probably by sitting on a committee, and being ignored by a wider range of people. That sort of thing would sap anyone's confidence. My confidence has grown over years of increasing involvement, with tremendous support from friends and colleagues in the survivor movement who knew what I was facing every step of the way.

His clients are probably drugged up to the eyeballs. People who have known me on depot injections, on cocktails of uppers, downers and mood stabilisers; people who have supported me through eighteen months of withdrawal against medical advice; people who've been through it themselves will understand. The drugs used in psychiatry can make it very difficult to articulate anything. The effects they can have on memory, concentration, even the mechanics of standing and speaking, make it very difficult to contribute with confidence. There was a time when I was on depot injections - it lasted two years - that I just wanted to stay in bed. I had precious little energy for day to day life. Participating in anything more demanding than making lunch would have been impossible. If I stood up too quickly, I would fall over. Not too impressive at the start of a speech!

I have been lucky. I have had the means and support to break out of a system that kept me silent. I believe that everyone has it in them to contribute to improving services. That doesn't necessarily mean hundreds of thousand of service users giving lectures, running workshops and writing articles! That is not the route for everyone. What is so obviously needed is training and skill sharing to enable people to contribute in their own way. Survivors Speak Out, MINDLINK, and the United Kingdom Advocacy Network have run joint training sessions to enable service users to become high quality trainers. Many of us spend a lot of time training service users and professionals so that they can move together towards a more collaborative service.

"Who do *you* represent...": the "do as I say not as I do" syndrome. I know that committees and meetings and conferences and planning teams are packed full of "representatives". I know that the culture into which we are drawn likes to see itself as "democratic", but how representative or democratic are they? I have had this accusation cast in my direction in a meeting in which I was the only individual who had actually been elected!

I cannot hope to represent the "user/survivor movement". Being chair of Survivors Speak Out does not entitle me to wield a trade union style block vote. It gives me a chance to air views that do not get heard either often enough or at a high enough level. Whilst the views I express are predominantly my own, I believe they do reflect widely held concerns. I spend most of my life with survivors and current and ex-service users. They are my friends, my colleagues, my lifeline. To most of the professionals I deal with they are clients, consumers, people with a mental illness, or worse.

It is this different relationship that entitles us to
speak or train without feeling the need to be
representative. We are a diverse bunch. We cut across
the boundaries of class and gender and culture that
still grip the "mental health" professions particularly
at the higher levels. I do not claim that the survivor
movement is a perfect model, but I would ask people
to look carefully at their own glass house before they
throw their "who do *you* represent" stones in my
direction.

Part Five

Involvement for Empowerment

Working for Change as a Service User

Gareth Walton

I'm 27 years old. I'm an AIDS diagnosed man. I'm now a registered disabled person, and I've been living on benefits in a council flat since I lost my job. I've been unemployed now for about two years. I was tested positive for the virus in 1986, then I was diagnosed as having AIDs in 1989. I was a successful interior designer for six years, working hard and I had a relationship. I was young, I was running marathons, I had a comfortable standard of living. But that was all taken away due to the issue of AIDS, and because of my infection, I virtually lost it all. I lost my job, I lost my flat, I lost my partner and I needed help.

Getting things together has taken a lot of hard work, and a lot of unnecessary waste of time. What am I now today? Well, it's a combination especially of family and friends taking care of me, and my social worker who is practical and very sensitive. I don't know what I would have done without her. I think everybody in my situation should be entitled to one, although I know they don't get it. It's needed my own perseverance over the medical profession, including its prejudices; my knowledge of the infection and the decision to be open about it, to fight while trying to retain my dignity. I have to be very open. I find not being open because of prejudice very difficult to cope with. I don't like lying. I've never liked keeping secrets. The reason I am who I am now is because I've had all these problems, and I'm proud of that.

I've had the experiences, and I'm strong enough at the moment to help other people coming up behind me so they don't have to waste time. Anger makes me want to do it as well. I've been very angry because I've seen lots of friends and colleagues and other people who've had lots of problems, trying to get help, trying to get food and money because they need these to survive, and they just don't get them.

I have a lot of experience with lots of organisations: Body Positive, the Lighthouse, Landmark and AIDS Mastery - that's a weekend where professionals and people with AIDS all try to find out more about the issues as equals, and I go along to support other people. I do the Body Positive helpline and counsel people on the telephone. It's the only one where you can ring up if you're HIV and be sure there's somebody HIV on the other end of the line. I volunteer, and I also receive help from these things that I need. I get satisfaction and I also get help.

I love to dance and that's the one way I can forget about other problems. It's very easy to go somewhere and just lose yourself, boogy all night. That makes me happier, that makes me normal, I can still do that, I'm not dead. I enjoy it so much, it's such a pleasure. And when I went back home to Yorkshire with my parents, I travelled twenty miles every day when I was on their farm to go swimming at the international pool in Leeds, and to have fish and chips from a special fish and chip shop. My mother used to think I was crazy. She said "I don't understand why you do it". I said "I enjoy it". She wants to know why I don't spend all the time with her. She loves me and she tries to do as much as she possibly can.

I get pleasure out of being with my family. But again there's also the feelings which I haven't used. I couldn't ejaculate for a year. I was very ill for three years, so I spent three years without anybody touching me at all. On the emotional side, on a friendship basis, I manage to get that touching now because I've have the confidence to go out and meet people. This has been very difficult and I've been rejected quite a few times because I have AIDS, because of my colostomy, my skin problems. Other people who haven't got any of those problems don't want to know me. I don't need that pressure. I deal with my illness first and not the pressure of somebody else saying "Oh, I'm sorry, but I can't cope with you." Oh well, I understand you can't cope with me, but I don't really understand because I can't cope with it myself.

What I want as a service user from organisations are basic simple things: communication, contact with people for help, information. You need somebody to be able to talk to. One of the things that's made my social worker good for me is that she's been through with me right from the beginning. She has been to my house. Where contacts change every ten minutes - that's no good to me. She gave me confidence.

My social worker introduced me to the Quality Assurance Group in Social Services. It's a Group which meets every month for people who are HIV and affected by AIDS within the Borough. We sit down in a nice room and very casually have a cup of tea or talk about issues, basically around the services provided within our Borough and any other problems as well. For example, I put forward at the Group the fact that there needs to be provision for home helps to work more sensitively with people with HIV. I know friends who've had real problems with home care workers because their attitudes have been terrible.

This Borough has the largest proportion of people in the country with HIV and AIDS. The Quality Assurance Group is something which has developed because we have a voice. When we ask for new services to be provided or for services to be updated, there's a unique opportunity to have some control. We're intelligent people. We're like everybody else. When we get angry and shout and have problems, we want to air them. And that's why this Group has actually been forced to develop.

We have a community worker who comes there every day, a wonderful chap. I can talk to him and he's very sensitive. He's a supporter for the Group. What makes him a good supporter is that he obviously works very hard and really believes in what he's doing, and he treats everybody equally. I feel just as good as him when I go to the meetings. That's really important to find in a professional. I'm not intimidated by him at all.

We get lots of other people who come down as well to the Group, social workers, other home care workers, people like that. They come along as people who offer us the service, to talk to us and just to be there. So the community worker is there, the people who have HIV or AIDS, and professionals come down now and then if an issue comes up and they want to talk about it with us. It's not a just meeting, although we do have minutes that are sent to us on what we talked about, which is very good. I think a record does need to be kept. It's a voluntary and flexible thing. You can go down there, stay for ten minutes and go off to have your hair done, or go to the doctor's - that's what's good about it.

People understand when you have more problems at some moment: that your priorities are somewhere else, that you're having to go to the doctor or whatever. The Quality Assurance Group understands that you can have good and bad times. I can meet other people, including people who use the service and have problems as well. I want to know why they've had problems, and if that will happen to me. I get to know about benefits and things like that. Just simple things. Things like the Independent Living Fund.

It's the best thing actually for people with HIV and AIDS at the moment within the system, but I've got criticisms about it too. The big problem is that for financial reasons a lot of things don't get done. As much as they can do without financial assistance they will try, but yet not very much gets done. But there are ways of getting cash, as I've seen from other groups in other areas. This Group is the best thing that which has happened to any borough in London as far as I know, but it still is not good enough.

We've had some successes. For instance, we've helped get an answering machine, a 24 hour answering machine, which is a direct line. We don't have to go through the Town Hall or anything like that. There's quite a few other things as well. We're discussing how to get one of the stalls on the market next to the vegetable stalls, to get information and leaflets out in the Borough, to just be there for people. We want to make HIV an issue for everybody in the Borough because it is an issue for everybody in the Borough. We also hear about what's happening in other parts of the Borough, about other groups that are being set up and follow them up. One group have a newsletter which they actually hand out, and that's interesting. I would like to find out more about it. I would like our Group to set one up as well, to send to people who have an HIV problem, a little magazine. The Quality Assurance Group is still developing and it's got far to go.

There are blueprints of user-led systems being worked up in some voluntary organisations. At most of their major meetings users are there, listening, joining in the conversations, involved in the management decisions. They're actually there. Body Positive for example is based on a self-help system so nobody actually gets paid to do anything except for things like the accounts. They're volunteers. It's in the control of people who are affected by HIV. In the social services things have always been decided by professionals. I'd like to see more say or more input by people who've got AIDS because they know about the problems.

I think it's very very important for the two areas - the statutory and the voluntary sector - to link up. You need the solid structure of the statutory services because the voluntary sector can be very difficult to get hold of. The statutory sector could learn a lot from the voluntary sector. You need to get the structure of the statutory sector organised in such a way that it can help people with HIV in the way in which the voluntary sector does.

I think it's very important for people to realise what AIDS is. I was always frightened to see somebody dying with AIDS, with pneumonia, with Karposi's sarcoma, with cancer, with any problem. But it's made me more aware. It's made me feel a lot better about myself. There are professional people in the statutory sector who don't have a clue what it's about. Lots of my friends ask me "Why do you do the telephone line?"; "Why do you go and see people with AIDS?" And I say that for me it's very important. And I think it's very important for professionals to do it as well. You have to be made aware of what the problem is, and where it could lead. Otherwise you just lose the view of what you're trying to help people with.

Service Users as Representatives

CHRIS HARRISON

In many areas of work, from participation on committees to training professionals, users of mental health services and disabled people generally are often accused of not being representative. Several factors need to be addressed by professionals if they wish to analyse this assertion more closely.

Firstly, many service users are now part of active self advocacy and support groups in the community, or members of representatives' committees such as patients' councils or day centre groups. They actively attempt to consult with fellow users to inform their contributions, whatever the issue. The elected user or users also feed back to their peers about their work. In short, representation and accountability feature very highly on the agenda of many active users.

Secondly, many professionals will concede that in a forum such as a planning meeting, they are not merely representing the views of their particular agency but also expressing a personal opinion. It would therefore impose a double standard on users if fellow committee members insist that they are "representative" all the time. In our experience, most champions of self-advocacy from the user perspective take pains to distinguish clearly between a collectively held opinion and a personal one. This often is not the case with professionals.

Finally, the growth in strength and experience of the disabled people's and user movements has enabled many members to acquire broad experience of working in many of the areas of decision making which affect them and their peers. Whether paid or unpaid, many service users are eminently well qualified to participate on equal terms with professionals and expect their contributions to be treated with respect and on merit.

INVOLVING OLDER PEOPLE

Many younger service users and sympathetic professionals express justified concern about the current lack of involvement of older people. Ageist stereotypes result in behaviour that excludes, demeans and marginalises them. Attempts, however, are being made to redress this unsatisfactory and unjust state of affairs. In our experience this takes two forms.

The first is through the actions of national and local pensioners' organisations. They are attempting to consult with, and raise issues relevant to, older people in local areas and, where possible, at national level. The second is through the use of the model of "user involvement" in specific agencies, which many younger people also champion actively.

Both cases give the lie to the notion that older people, whatever their apparent degree of impairment, are unable or unwilling to express opinions about decisions which affect them in small or large ways. I would suggest that both the user movement and established organisations can and should learn from these successful examples, change their practice and encourage the empowerment of older service users.

RESOURCES

When either service users or providers discuss what changes could or should be made, the question of human and financial resources is always raised. We live in a climate, at present, where such resources are inadequate and unevenly distributed. However, we have to avoid allowing this to get in the way of active dialogue about how services can be restructured and made more responsive and accountable.

Though many of us are aware of the shortfalls of community care legislation and resource allocation, we must still take the opportunity to consider not merely what we would do if resources were more plentiful, but also how they are currently allocated and by whom they are controlled. The current situation, not least for users from black and ethnic minorities, makes it a battle to obtain any service at all, let alone have a greater say in how that service can be more sensitively delivered.

Service users still face the frustrations of being denied the right to receive and participate in the provision of services, not only because of resource scarcities but also because many stakeholders with power, including national government, are reluctant to contemplate a more equal distribution.

Though there needs to be a joint strategy by the disability and user movements to campaign for more provision, resources even at current levels can provide a basis for differently run and more sensitive services. That's why it's crucial to campaign for service users to be involved now, as well as pressing for more resources for the future. Otherwise service users will continue to be at the back of the queue, waiting in vain for the day when national and local politicians see the light and make the necessary changes themselves.

The Victim of Success: A Black Worker's Experience of the Voluntary Sector

HARDEESH K. RAI

INTRODUCTION

Many people need support from the voluntary or statutory services, and miss out either because the services are not accessible to them or because they do not meet their particular needs. In Southall, where I was employed in a voluntary organisation as a community worker to support families who had children with special needs and who were mostly Asians, this situation occurred all too frequently. Southall, in the London Borough of Ealing, is a notably multicultural area: 80% of people are Sikhs, Hindus or Muslims of Asian origin. The rest belong to European, Chinese, Afro-Caribbean or Somali communities.

I joined the voluntary organisation, which specialises in family services, in April 1986 when it was in its infancy: five months old and in contact with only 11 families. I was assured that other families who had children with special needs would be referred to me by social workers, health visitors, schools and other statutory and voluntary agencies based in the area. From previous experience I was well aware that welfare services largely ignored and failed to deal with the needs of Asian people because of lack of understanding of their language, culture, religion and values. Stereotypes and myths about Asian people are widespread among monolingual and monocultural workers. My employers were to be congratulated in setting up a project to support black families. Unfortunately they were unaware of the realities of working with such communities, and the danger that a community worker would get sandwiched between local realities and established service structures.

Service users who are not articulate in expressing their needs often don't get the services available because their involvement at the planning level is virtually nil and decisions are made by small groups of officers who have little understanding about them. It has to be remembered that service users may well be able to express their views in their own languages, but planners ignore them because they - Asians or other people whose natural language is not English - lack confidence in English. This results in monolingual professionals causing more problems, rather than solving the existing ones.

As a black woman I knew from the beginning that this work was not going to be easy. I could not see myself being neutral about the needs of Asian families and knew I might be considered to be taking sides. But I did not see how I could collude with the expectations of a system controlled by people who had never really thought about such families.

FIRST STEPS

After waiting for referrals for two months with increasing desperation, I started writing to various agencies and professionals whom by then I knew by name, requesting an appointment to introduce myself and explain the support the project could provide to families with children with special needs, and emphasising that families from all races and backgrounds were welcome. I received only one reply, from the headteacher of a special school. There are four special schools around Southall where over 40% of the children are from black families - Asians and Afro-Caribbeans. The failure of response from the other agencies I wrote to, together with the negative attitudes I encountered from a number of individual professionals, gave an indication of the general lack of understanding about the needs of black people. I could see a rough road ahead.

The head teacher however did arrange a meeting, and I found her very willing to look into the issues concerning Asian parents and their children's welfare. She agreed to send copies of my introductory letter to families throughout her school, and over 70 replied within the following two weeks. I made home visits to them all, and the workload began to get heavier and more interesting day by day. The common concern was lack of information about and access to services such as disability benefits, respite care, social work support, parental involvement in education, and health care in regard to ante-natal and post-natal provision in the local hospital and clinics.

More specifically:

• None of the families had heard of invalid care allowance. This benefit was granted to mothers regardless of their husband's income in 1984.

- Only 40 families out of 70 were claiming attendance allowance.

- Thirty children were entitled to mobility allowance, but parents had received no information from any of the statutory workers.

- Twenty families were receiving child benefit only, and were not aware of other allowances.

- None of the families were sure about what to expect from social workers or health visitors.

In addition, respite care was unknown to all the families, though this service had existed for the previous four years in Ealing. For example, an Asian mother, a widow with four children, herself disabled, had a son with severe learning difficulties, but received no support. Soon after her bereavement, she had been visited by a social worker and offered respite care for her son. The meaning of respite care was not explained, and the mother, believing the intention was to take her son away on a permanent basis, refused. Her file was closed and she was left to cope on her own until I became involved four years later.

Through similar case work it became apparent that a large residential centre for children with special needs in Southall was being used almost exclusively by white families from outside the area. The centre's policy was to encourage long term admissions, inappropriate for Asian families interested in a short term, flexible service. Campaigning on this issue resulted in the centre offering short term and emergency care. A similar situation arose with a

Social Services respite care scheme recruiting families as carers for children with special needs. Because no Asians were involved as carers, the service was not taken up by Asian families. A six week training course arranged with Social Services for Asian carers drew 14 Asian women participants who then became carers.

In 1988 it emerged that although grants were available for holidays for disabled persons, this information had not been circulated to black organisations. After lobbying the Social Services Department, the project obtained funding to take children on holidays, but there was a discrepancy between the amounts allocated to white and black groups. Later on, after discussions with the Department, this was resolved. But it seems that if black people don't fight for their share, they don't get it.

USER INVOLVEMENT

The strongest barrier between Social Services and the community was the lack of understanding about language, culture and values. In 1988 a large meeting was arranged between the Social Services Department and black families. Parents were encouraged to express their problems in their own language through interpreters, and most spoke up about the issues which concerned them. This was a breach in the concrete wall round the system, and a shock for the professionals who had fed the Department with their own stereotypical assumptions about the needs of black people. As a result the Director of Social Services promised to look into current policies and provision.

Some time afterwards, I was invited by the Social

Services Department to participate in various meetings and panels in an advisory capacity. I appreciated this but was very wary of being used as a "token" representative of all the minority ethnic communities in the area, so I asked for assurance from the chair of the Special Needs Advisory Panel that my involvement would indeed be taken into consideration in planning respite care and day care provision. But it was a tough struggle passing the message through to the service providers. Often my presence was felt to be nothing but a trouble, and such attitudes became part and parcel of my daily work and life.

Change is becoming evident in some services, but it very much depends on individual front-line workers or managers. Some recognise the circumstances which create problems and some create circumstances which result in further problems. The new community care legislation might bring some improvement for black communities but as yet the approaches to involving them in the planning level of services are not convincing.

EDUCATION

My own involvement extended beyond Social Services to the Education Department. The assessment and statementing procedures which categorise children as having special educational needs create a number problems for black parents and their children. Many professionals are aware of these needs in theory but find it difficult to put this into practice. The 1981 Education Act outlines the procedures for assessing children whose needs are, or probably are, such as to require local education authorities to determine special provision. The Act also requires information to be conveyed in "straightforward language" to parents so that they can take further action if necessary, and states that "the importance of parents' contributions should be pointed out". But the legal aspects of the statementing process are frequently disregarded in cases concerning black children and families.

In Southall, for example, Asian parents were seldom given any explanation why their children were being assessed and statemented, or told about their rights. Most decisions were made by professionals who ignored the notion of parental involvement. Even when parents disagreed with a decision, their objections were not recognised and excuses made instead to avoid complications. Moreover, information was not made available in Asian languages and no translation facility was provided. This failure to simplify professional jargon was a direct contravention of section 5 of the Act.

After assessment parents were not offered a choice of school or informed about how a special school could help their children. In such schools no mother tongue provision was available nor were there any arrangements for assessing children in their mother tongue, though some professionals would have welcomed this. When parents attended the annual children's reviews held by schools they found that reports by staff on their child's educational development were written in professional jargon using incomprehensible terms such as "cognitive skills, motorability, wider gate".

Parents would ask me to accompany them to provide support but I had to obtain official school permission despite the parents' request. Although I was present in a supportive capacity, professionals would insist on designating me as an interpreter, and it took almost three years of personal campaigning before they viewed my involvement as anything other than a "problem". The best solution for them was simply to avoid me and not inform me about forthcoming meetings.

There were many instances of children being wrongly allocated to special schools or nurseries because they could not be assessed in their own language. In 1985 before I became involved, a three year old Asian girl with impaired hearing was assessed and placed in a special day nursery. The parents were not informed that she had been statemented as speech impaired. When I visited the nursery in 1986 she was happy to see me, sat in my lap and told me vividly about her mother, the clothes she wore, her aunty, her family and so on. The white nursery nurse was taken aback to see the little girl engaging in a lengthy conversation. Because she could not speak English, she had been classified as "speech impaired". Even after the child guidance centre was informed of this grotesque mis-diagnosis, it took nearly a year to transfer the girl to an appropriate group in another school.

In another case, a special secondary school failed to recognise that a 15 year old boy possessed skills to respond to verbal stimuli, because he failed to react when addressed in English. When I joked with him in his own language, he laughed, made gestures with his eyes and gesticulated with his arms. Such examples demonstrate why my involvement in the statementing process of black children became essential in providing fair treatment in accordance within the existing regulations (Rai, 1990).

TRANSLATION

As increasing numbers of families joined the project, I became involved in other areas. Many families required information in their own language, but here I was left on my own by my organisation who felt that since none of their other projects had shown the need for such a service, it was not essential in Southall. However none of the other projects involved mostly Asian families or employed Asian workers. The Southall project was the first to do so - employing me full time and a part time administrator. I was allowed to go ahead in making provision, if I could raise funds on my own. With the pressures of my existing workload, I felt I was being sandwiched between the needs of the community, lack of funds and the brick wall of the system.

After many applications to various charities, a small fund was made available. Information on welfare rights and assessment and statementing procedures for children with special educational needs was needed urgently. This was translated into four Asian languages - Punjabi, Hindi, Urdu and Gujurati, the main languages used in the area. The translated information was widely taken up, not only locally but also by statutory agencies and voluntary organisations all over the country.

Now that everyone could understand their rights, I was loaded down with the extra work of filling in the benefit forms, making applications for disability allowances and appealing for backdated claims. Two issues arose here. Firstly, the administrator was only employed part-time and had no training on welfare rights. Secondly, my organisation had no funds to provide such training, so in a way I was punished for my own initiative.

HEALTH SERVICES

The problems created by lack of appropriate social services and special education provision were compounded by the inadequacies of the health services. Lack of thought on the part of doctors prevented them from treating Asian mothers who gave birth to children with special needs sympathetically. Their stereotyped views of Asian culture resulted in many instances when such mothers were put in awkward situations because they could not speak English (Rai, 1991).

An Asian mother gave birth to a Downs syndrome child in a local hospital. The baby was kept in a special baby unit for three days, but no-one explained to the mother why and she was very distressed. Eventually, the ward sister called an Asian cleaner to explain that the baby was a "Mongol" and that she could not take him in her lap. Now firstly, the term "Mongol" is derogatory and no longer used any more. Secondly, how could a cleaner be expected to counsel a woman in distress? When I was informed by the family, I went to the hospital. The mother burst out crying and expressed her helplessness in dealing with doctors and other nursing staff. I asked the ward sister if I could see the doctor concerned, and the look she gave me made me realise she could not believe such a request from an Asian woman. It was obvious that she found it hard to agree but could not refuse because of my politeness and concern, and she called in the doctor. I asked about the mother and baby, and was told that she was given no explanation in case she became "hysterical", causing emotional distress and creating problems for staff.

The issue arises time and time again: counselling services are available for white and middle class mothers but not for those Asian mothers who desperately need them. Are Asian people supposed not to have feelings? No wonder mental health institutions are full of black patients.

THE ROLE OF BLACK WORKERS

Different problems also arose because of my position as a black worker in a white organisation. When Asian workers are employed as token gestures by statutory and voluntary agencies, they are expected to enhance the organisation's status and achieve maximum results with minimum resources. Most work in isolation, under pressure, with no support from their superiors. They find themselves in the middle of a tangled web and gain nothing for themselves in terms of promotion or recognition of their work and struggles. When they achieve real improvements for service users, they become victims of their own success. Employers feel threatened and withdraw endorsement just as the workload increases.

For example, when I was appointed in Southall my advertised job title was as "community worker", and paid at that rate. I was responsible for developing the project according to the needs of local families. A similar project was based in the Ealing area, where almost all the families were white. Though both projects had the same aims and objectives, the needs and values of the local families differed tremendously. In Southall, families belong to different cultures, backgrounds and languages and their values are

different from those of white families. After two years,
I found that my white colleague's post in Ealing,
where she did not have to face any of my problems,
carried the title "area coordinator" instead of
community worker, and was on a higher salary scale.
The discrepancy in our titles, I was told, was because
she was playing "a vital role" within the Borough in
supporting families.

Both of us were working on the same level, but I had
the additional responsibilities of translating
information and supporting families in maintaining
their cultural and religious values. I questioned this
and caused problems. I lost friends in the
organisation. After prolonged reluctance I was given
the title of "project coordinator" but the discrepancy
in salary was never solved. As a result, I was seen to
be causing trouble for the organisation. Whenever
black workers prove their ability, white employers
feel threatened and try to marginalise them. This
leaves us facing the same isolation, racism, prejudice
and discrimination as the communities we work with.

Black workers get tangled up in the system just as
much as the people they try to support. Commonplace
assumptions about Asian families are invoked to
justify minimal or non-involvement of specialist
Asian workers, and expressed in clichés such as:

- "Asian people do not join in self-help groups";

- "Asian families do not welcome interference from
  outsiders";

- "black people choose not to take up the services
  available to them";

- "the extended family is all the support they need";

- "they should consider themselves lucky to be in England";

- "Asian families try to milk the state by claiming disability benefits for their children."

These are actual comments recorded from two professionals in Southall, an education social worker and a health worker.

OUTCOMES

All this creates many problems for Asian families:

- Black people do not take advantage of the present system because they cannot - planning and delivery of services is formulated to exclude them. Service providers seem to be reluctant to recognise this, because it is more convenient to stick with convenient stereotypes than to work on issues which create difficulties.

- Social services blame black families because they do not use "resources" such as fostering, adoption or respite care. But efforts are seldom made to explain in their own languages the benefits available and how to access them.

- Lack of proper information and consultation leads to services based on incorrect assumptions.

As project coordinator, I encountered numerous problems. After nearly six years of struggle, most agencies - education, social services and health services - recognised the validity of my role but within my own organisation I felt isolated and alienated from other workers, relegated to a second class status because of my colour and cultural differences. The main reasons were very limited contact with other workers in the organisation, no other black staff to share problems with, overwork and lack of recognition by my superiors. Only through support from workers elsewhere, parents and friends did I manage to achieve my aims and objectives. After six years, I left the project to study full time for a qualification in social work.

Most black workers become victims of the circumstances in which they try to realise their aspirations. They are attracted by jobs offering opportunities to work with minority ethnic groups. They feel their efforts might be able to change the stereotyped views held by service providers. But in practice they experience the negativity of employers who lack knowledge of the linguistic and cultural values of black people and fail to support black workers. Their efforts to achieve real change thus become their own problems. However in my case, success in overcoming the difficulties of developing the project gave me a firm determination to keep on fighting for equality and justice.

Currently I am a member of the Asian Parents and Carers Association, whose role is to advocate for services for black teenagers with special needs. At present, services tend to ignore Asian family values and thus alienate potential users. For me this is a unique opportunity to be involved with the community whose problems I have been sharing for many years.

A Vision for the Future

Viv Lindow

Giving a vision for the future is a tall order. Weather forecasters, with their panoply of equipment and scientific mystery, cannot tell us much about the day after tomorrow. But as a psychiatric survivor perhaps I have more chance. We are good at visions.

Where do we start from? Today we have people begging on the streets. We have people living in cardboard boxes and other temporary shelters. These examples of community living are direct consequences of social and economic policies. They were not seen here during my childhood. Begging and living in temporary shelters were misrepresented to me at school as being typical of lifestyles in the "less civilized" countries on the pink part of the British imperial map.

Government and the established professions have had their chance and they have failed us. My vision for the future develops from initiatives by users of community care services.

A psychiatric in-patient in the Bronx, New York, had a "job" in the hospital kitchen. He saw the huge level of waste there and the homeless people who lived around the hospital. At ward level, it was decided to save food that would otherwise be returned to the kitchen, and distribute it nearby. That was in 1984.

The project that arose from this user-initiative, Share Your Bounty, now employs 18 current and former

users of the Bronx Psychiatric Centre, and is directed
by a survivor. About half the workers have
themselves been homeless. They collect food from
retailers and distribute it directly to people who are
unwilling to contact establishment shelters and food
distribution points (Montes, Masiello and Masiello,
1990).

RELEVANCE AND EFFICIENCY

Share Your Bounty has the typical characteristics of
user-controlled services. It is a partnership among
equals that attracts its users. It addresses the real
needs and immediate concerns of service users. The
top three concerns of most long-term mental health
services users are:

* poverty
* homelessness
* unemployment.

These are our concerns, yet they consult us about the
colour of the curtains in the day centre. They call that
"user involvement".

WORKING SEPARATELY AND TOGETHER

One continuing feature of the lives of people who need
support to live equal lives in the community is that,
once we have shown such a need, this marks us for
exclusion from mainstream society. It remains legal
to discriminate against us in various ways. We are
not encouraged to set up our own alternatives.
Instead expert professionals, the purchasers and
planners, make a lot of money out of presuming to
know best about our needs.

Using a new perspective, our perspective, many of us

would ask "What resources do we need to give us lives of equal quality to people who are not impaired?" Give service users some of these resources, and we will surprise you by how well we get on with "care in the community". Involve us in resource allocation, and you may be surprised to hear that we never wanted that day centre. That is why we were not enthusiastic about selecting the colour of the curtains.

Through lack of opportunity and discrimination, many more of us live on benefits than want to. Service users certainly understand about scarce resources and rationing. We can hardly do worse than what has been done so far by professional people alone deciding what is the best use of these resources.

Users of community care services have many tasks to do. We need resources to do them. Some activities we will undertake separately according to our own concerns. Elders, people with learning difficulties, disabled people, individuals who test HIV positive, people with AIDS and psychiatric survivors all have expertise in our own needs and rights. Black and white people, women and men, lesbians, gay men, and heterosexual people within these and other groups - all are concerned with issues in which we specialise.

There will be difficulties. Like any group of humans, we have our empire-builders who seek to speak for everyone. They deny the legitimacy of each group speaking about its own issues. As a counterbalance, much of the strength of oppressed groups lies in a preference for flattened hierarchies. Because we have ourselves experienced oppression by the majority, we wish to include rather than exclude the minority voice.

The various disadvantaged groups in society do have issues in common, not least the need for anti-discrimination legislation. On these issues, we can learn to work together without oppressing each other. We can fight together for our human rights in this unequal society.

TARGETING THOSE WITH POWER

As change-agents for the future, we can concentrate on lobbying those who have power. We can continue to learn to use the media and influence government. We must oppose those who misuse their power to control our lives. Another main focus will be consciousness raising among our own groups. There are still too many people who accept paternalistic services, and are grateful to be noticed at all. We can let them know that they deserve better.

The media

The media, especially television, have a total lack of interest in showing some points of view. Mental health service users' issues are rarely touched: those concerning black psychiatric survivors even more rarely. Disadvantaged older people hardly get a fair hearing. Rightly, deaf people do get some air time: people with other impairments increasingly so. We want our voices to have equal weight with those of the "experts". We know rather more about the subject of community living in a discriminated group than they do.

But why should we fit in with media standards of visual acceptability and white anglo-saxon communication skills? As well as having time to air our own issues, we want to be represented on television and in the press doing the same range of things as everyone else. Other discriminated groups, especially women, Asian and black people, and people with regional dialects have shown how appearing in ordinary roles on television raises the prestige of and perceptions about formerly excluded groups of people.

One key to achieving power in moving towards user-led services will be our growing confidence in our own expertise. We do not need mis-trained professional people interpreting us to decision-makers. One particularly irritating characteristic of experts is the confidence with which they make their pronouncements about us. We can make equally confident and much more accurate observations. We can build on the work of the current pioneers. More of us can become media experts.

Medical and para-medical power

The old asylums for people with learning difficulties and people diagnosed and treated as "mentally ill" were introduced with great confidence, as the humane breakthrough that would protect and care for us. Hospital care for elders and disabled people of all ages is misrepresented in the same way. A humane breakthrough? No, rather powerbases for doctors and other professional people to command us, cow us and ruin our lives.

Don't let them get away with it again. There is no likelihood that moving psychiatrists and paramedics to different settings in the community will be an improvement. Their calls for increased legislation for drugging citizens in their own homes, for Community Supervision Orders under the Mental Health Act, show clearly that they have learned nothing about humanity or human rights from the hospital experience.

While professionals try to ignore the contradictions between their social control tactics, human rights and user-friendly services, we will draw this to the attention of anyone who will listen. The issue of using drugs for social control of certain groups of people has received some media attention, but many others seem to be so disregarded that the most brain-damaging drugs are thought fair enough for us (Breggin, 1991).

Nor are doctors the only people engaged in obvious social control. I have twice recently heard of psychologists in unconnected services who worked out behaviour-control regimes in residential "homes" *without meeting the person concerned*. One recipient was an older mental health service user: another a woman with learning difficulties. Clearly the psychologists were serving the staff by controlling residents' inconvenient behaviour rather than serving the people themselves.

These people must be targeted with our strenuous opposition. Those of us who are fortunate enough to have escaped - for now, anyway - the power of the medical professions are free to do this without fear of reprisal. If our future is to be in our own hands, we must push and push to get this unacceptable face of "care" in the community publicised and stopped. If we do not do this, the vision for the future is a doctor's delight, and a continuation of the nightmare for many of us.

Professional training

The nightmare will only recede if there are fundamental changes in the way we are served in the community. Much more is needed than the occasional appearance of token service users in the discussions of the purchasers and providers. And more than the token interest of the planners of services in "consulting" us.

The great majority of community service providers today have a wholly inappropriate training. Many of their skills are irrelevant to service users' concerns. Their attitudes and practices are often pompous, patronising and paternalistic.

All training courses need a total overhaul. Service users who have experienced the products of existing training should have a real input into the curriculum and the content of new courses, both as planners and as trainers.

National and local government

The last crucial group of powerful people to be targeted if we are to seize better futures are those who hold the money. These are mainly those who have political power, and their paid officers.

We need resources to start to take on new leadership roles in community care. The national groups started by members of the various disability groups need secure funding at a level that recognises the importance of the tasks we have to do. These tasks are many and various, but good community services will not be realised unless we can secure proper money.

Some of these tasks I have mentioned: reaching out to enable other service users to revalue themselves and join the equality enterprise; becoming planners and trainers; lobbying government for change; becoming media experts. The product of these activities could be widespread provision of appropriate and effective services.

Above all else, we need resources to meet together, locally and nationally, and to reach out to those we have not yet met. Resources for local and national user groups are the essential foundation for building user-led services. Without them, we cannot work together for change.

Concentrating on people more powerful than ourselves can be discouraging for us. They do not yield easily, whatever their rhetoric about user participation and needs-led services. I have moments of despair about working so hard and not seeming to get anywhere in seeking improved attitudes and services for us psychiatric survivors. My source of hope is in the expanding user movement. All those people out there who could revalue themselves and have a better future if only we can reach them. They can join us in the struggle.

Money needs to move up the line towards those it is meant to benefit. Those who know least how to use resources to our advantage are given large salaries for stating their opinions. At the same time, they act as gatekeepers who prevent us from taking responsibility for our own care.

POPULAR SERVICES

Of all the stakeholders in building more appropriate community care, we service users have the least money and the greatest expertise. Independent Living and other user-controlled schemes are a resounding success with their users. As well as giving us the dignity of remaining in control of our destiny, user-led services can reach the parts of society that other services cannot reach. Share Your Bounty and many other user-controlled services in North America show the possibility of popular services that attract formerly intractable individuals.

What an idea! Services that are popular, that attract users, are relevant to what we say we need. Services that serve. Why do these descriptions sound so strange to those of us who only have the choice of existing services, or nothing?

Huge amounts of cash, though not enough, given the oppressiveness of most existing services, are going into providing advocacy projects to protect the rights of recipients of health and social services community care arrangements. How irrational this seems once you grasp the idea that moving resources from unpopular services into the hands of these same recipients could transform the scene.

Service users as purchasers. Service user as providers. Service users with individual budgets and the power of the purse. They would buy the skills of existing professionals that they find useful. They would join together to provide services as part of the government's "mixed economy of care". Advocacy services would still be needed, but on a far smaller scale.

User-controlled services waste little money because we know our needs. With enough resources we can retain control of our lives. We can stop being seen as social problems: we become part of the solution. Pass the money along to us, and the vision of community services that really serve will soon be realised.

References

Marian Barnes, (1993), "Introducing New Stakeholders - User and Research Interests in Evaluative Research: A Discussion of Methods Used to Evaluate the Birmingham Community Care Special Action Project", *Policy and Politics*, Vol.21, No.1, pp.47-58.

Marian Barnes and Gerald Wistow, (1992), *Partnership and Empowerment: Involving Carers in Monitoring Outcomes of the Consultations,* A Final Report from the Evaluation of the Birmingham Community Care Special Action Project, Nuffield Institute for Health Service Studies.

Peter Beresford and Suzy Croft, (1993), *Citizen Involvement: A Practical Guide for Change,* Macmillan.

Peter Breggin, (1993), *Toxic Psychiatry: A Psychiatrist Speaks Out,* Fontana, London

Suzy Croft and Peter Beresford, (1979), *Community Control of Social Services Departments,* Battersea Community Action.

Suzy Croft and Peter Beresford, (1992), "The Politics of Participation", *Critical Social Policy*, (35), Autumn, pp. 20-44.

Michael Dunne, (1992), *Recruiting and Employing a Personal Care Worker,* Disablement Income Group.

Kathryn Ellis, (1993), *Squaring the Circle: User and Carer Participation in Needs Assessment*, Joseph Rowntree Foundation/*Community Care*.

Hampshire Centre for Independent Living, (1987), *The Source Book Towards Independent Living,* Hampshire Centre for Independent Living.

Tessa Harding, (1992), *Great Expectations...and Spending on Social Services,* Policy Forum Paper No 1, National Institute for Social Work.

Bill Jordan, (1975), "Is the Client a Fellow Citizen?", *Social Work Today*, 30th October.

Jenny Morris, (1993), *Community Care or Independent Living?*, Joseph Rowntree Foundation/ *Community Care*.

E. Montes, P. Masiello and B. Masiello, (1990), "Patients Helping Themselves by Helping the Homeless: Share Your Bounty, the Friends of the Homeless Project", *Hospital and Community Psychiatry*, Vol.41, No.10.

John O'Brien, (1986), "A Guide to Personal Futures Planning" in G.T. Bellamy and B. Wilcox (eds), *A Comprehensive Guide to the Activities Catalog: An Alternative Curriculum for Youth and Adults with Severe Disabilities*, Paul J.H. Brookes.

Michael Oliver, (1990), *The Politics of Disablement*, Macmillan.

Mike Oliver, (1991-2), Review of: Naomi Connelly, *Raising Voices: Social Services Departments and People with Disabilities*, Policy Studies Institute, 1990, *Critical Social Policy*, (33), Winter, pp.115-116.

Phyllida Parsloe and Olive Stevenson, (1993), *Community Care and Empowerment*, Joseph Rowntree Foundation/*Community Care*.

Hardeesh Rai, (1990), "Asian Children with Special Needs", *Multicultural Teaching*, Vol.9, No.1.

Hardeesh Rai, (1991), *Who Really Cares?* Report by London Voluntary Services Council, LVSC.

Social Services Inspectorate (1991), *Care Management and Assessment: Managers' Guide*, HMSO.

Wagner Development Group, (1993), *Positive Answers,* HMSO.

Andrea Whittaker, Simon Gardner and Joyce Kershaw, (1991), *Service Evaluation by People with Learning Difficulties*, King's Fund Centre.

Helpful Material

Association of Metropolitan Authorities, (1991), *Quality and Contracts in the Personal Social Services*, London, Association of Metropolitan Authorities.

Colin Barnes, (1991), *Disabled People in Britain and Discrimination: A Case for Anti-Discrimination Legislation,* London, Hurst and Company, University of Calgary Press/ British Council of Organisations of Disabled People.

Marian Barnes and Gerald Wistow, (eds), (1992), *Researching User Involvement*, Leeds, Nuffield Institute for Health Services Studies, University of Leeds.

Peter Beresford and Suzy Croft, (1993), *Citizen Involvement: A Practical Guide for Change*, London, Macmillan.*

Judi Chamberlin, (1988), *On Our Own: Patient-Controlled Alternatives to the Mental Health System,* London, MIND.

Suzy Croft and Peter Beresford, (1993), *Getting Involved: A Practical Manual,* London, Open Services Project/Joseph Rowntree Foundation.*

Kathryn Ellis, (1993), *Squaring the Circle: User and Carer Participation in Needs Assessment*, York, Joseph Rowntree Foundation/*Community Care*.

Hampshire Centre for Independent Living, (1987), *The Source Book Towards Independent Living,* Hampshire Centre for Independent Living.

Tessa Harding and Angela Upton, (1991), *User Involvement in Social Services: An Annotated Bibliography,* London, National Institute for Social Work.

Mental Health Media Council, (1993), *From Anger to Action: Advocacy, Empowerment and Mental Health,* (Video), London, Mental Health Media Council.

Jenny Morris, (1993), *Community Care or Independent Living?,* York, Joseph Rowntree Foundation/*Community Care.*

Jenny Morris and Vivien Lindow, (1993), *User Participation in Community Care Services,* London, Department of Health Community Care Support Force.*

Jim Read and Jan Wallcraft, (1992), *Guidelines for Empowering Users of Mental Health Services,* London, MIND Publications/COHSE, The Health Care Union.

Randall Smith, Lucy Gastor, Lyn Harrison, Linda Martin, Robin Means, Peter Thistlethwaite, (1993), *Working Together for Better Community Care,* Bristol, School of Advanced Urban Studies, University of Bristol.

Survivors Speak Out, *Self-Advocacy Pack*, (1993), (revised edition), London, Survivors Speak Out.

Catherine Thompson, (ed), 1991, *Changing the Balance: Power and People Who Use Services*, London, Community Care Project, National Council for Voluntary Organisations.

User Centred Services Group, (1993), *Building Bridges Between People Who Use and People Who Provide Services*, London, National Institute for Social Work.*

Liz Winn, (ed), (1990), *Power to the People: The Key to Responsive Services in Health and Social Care*, London, King's Fund Centre.

Andrea Whittaker, Simon Gardner and Joyce Kershaw, (1991), *Service Evaluation by People with Learning Difficulties*, London, King's Fund Centre.

Richard Wood, (1991), *Speaking Up for Yourself: Putting Advocacy into Practice,* London, Age Concern, England.

Also available in audio-cassette form.

The Authors

Betty Asafu-Adjaye co-presented one of the workshops at the original conference *A Challenge to Change.*

Avenue Road Centre Quality Action Group in the London Borough of Newham brought together a number of people. Peter Allen, Head of Psychology Services in Newham, acted as a co-ordinator of the Group. Other participants included Paul Blake and Mary Pannett, who are both service users; Ruth Cochrane from Newham Community College; Jay Lewis from the Avenue Resource Centre; Angela Charrington, an occupational therapist; and over the life of the Group other people interested in local day provision and the possible benefit of establishing a Quality Action Group.

Ingrid Barker is currently Unit General Manager of Croydon Mental Health Unit and a Consultant with the Centre for Mental Health Services Development. Previously she was Contracts Manager with Newcastle Health Authority. A trained social worker, she has worked mainly in the voluntary sector and has been closely involved with the user movement in mental health since 1985.

Marian Barnes has worked in research and development posts, social services departments as well as in universities. Her particular interests are in community care, user involvement and mental health. Her current work includes work with Age Concern, Scotland on a project to establish user panels of frail elderly people, and research looking at

"Consumerism and citizenship amongst users of health and social care services."

Peter Beresford works with Open Services Project and is a senior lecturer in social policy at West London Institute, College of Brunel University. He is a member of Survivors Speak Out. He has a longstanding involvement in issues of participation and empowerment as a service user, worker, researcher and through his involvement in community action. He is author of many publications on the subject, most recently *Citizen Involvement: A Practical Guide for Change* (Macmillan, 1993).

Julie Bingham is a member of Oxfordshire Pensioners Action Group. Prior to retirement she worked in the Civil Service and was very active in the Trade Union Movement. Post-retirement she remains politically active. She was one of the first pensioners to enrol as a student at Ruskin College, Oxford.

Jane Campbell is an honours graduate of the University of Hertfordshire, with an MA in Political History. She worked briefly for the Royal Association for Disability and Rehabilitation before joining the Greater London Council Disability Unit. After a spell as Principal Disability Advisor to the London Borough of Hounslow, she was recruited to her current post as Joint Director of Training at the Disability Resource Team. Her training schemes have resulted in the establishment of the National Register of Disabled Consultants and Trainers. Jane is also co-chair of the British Council of Organisations of Disabled People, and is actively involved in national campaigns.

Jackie Downer is a Black woman with learning difficulties who currently works as a trainer and self-advocacy development worker. Jackie has facilitated conference workshops and has been a speaker at conferences. She supports and advises self-advocacy groups and does empowerment work directly with service users. Jackie does not speak for all service users but can offer her own experience in looking at issues that affect users of services. Jackie is a member of the Black Disability Forum and is active in local disability issues in South London.

Kathryn Ellis is currently a lecturer in social policy at the University of Luton. She carried out research on assessment practice whilst a research fellow at the University of Birmingham, prior to which she worked for several years in the voluntary sector.

Peter Ferns is a Black, non-disabled man who is a qualified social worker with over twelve years experience in services for people with learning difficulties and in the field of mental health. He has over eight years experience in training and consultancy work specialising in community care, learning difficulties, mental health, race equality and social work education. He has been an adviser to Black self-advocacy groups.

Bob Findlay worked for Birmingham Social Services Department from 1990 to 1992. At present he is Director of the Birmingham Information Federation. He founded the Birmingham Disability Rights Group and now represents them within the British Council of Organisations of Disabled People. He is a poet, comedian and West Bromwich Albion supporter.

Lorraine Gradwell is a disabled woman with two children. She is the joint honorary secretary of the Greater Manchester Coalition of Disabled People. From December 1986 until December 1992 Lorraine was a Coalition employee, initially as a development worker but for the last three years as Team Leader. Lorraine currently organises the joint-funded. Health for All initiative in Manchester.

Tessa Harding is a consultant at the National Institute for Social Work, with responsibility for policy development and a number of projects on user involvement and user-led services. She previously worked for three local authorities and the National Council for Voluntary Organisations. She is the author/editor of a number of publications, including *Great Expectations...and Spending on Social Services* and *Who Owns Welfare?* (National Institute for Social Work, 1992). She obtained a Harkness Fellowship for 1993/4 to study in the USA, on entitlement to social care for older people and other adults.

Frances Hasler started her career in the National Health Service, then worked at Spinal Injuries Association as Welfare/Development Officer, including setting up a nationwide, user-led personal assistance service. She moved in 1985 to Islington Disablement Association, a community based organisation. Appointed Director of the Greater London Association of Disabled People in 1990, she helped the organisation to become "user-led". She has extensive experience of developing voluntary sector services and is adviser to various research projects. She is a member of the Prince of Wales Advisory Group on Disability.

Anne James is a qualified social worker with considerable experience in community development. She first became involved with older people's issues in 1987 when working as a community development worker for Social Services in Oxford City. During that time she worked with the Pensioners Action Group on a number of projects including Oxford's Agewell projects. In 1990 she joined the Social Services Community Care Planning Team and co-wrote and edited Oxfordshire's first community care plan.

David Keay is Chair of Survivors Speak Out.

Joyce Kershaw is Secretary and Treasurer of Huddersfield People First. The group began in August 1985 and since then has come a long way. Joyce gives talks at many different places, such as hospitals and universities, and speaks at conferences. Joyce says, "I don't take no for an answer. I fight for my rights. I also try to be an advocate and help other people by speaking up for their rights. This is not always easy, but I enjoy this kind of work."

Viv Lindow is a psychiatric system survivor who works as a consultant, trainer and researcher in service user participation and other mental health matters. She has recently finished a research project funded by the Joseph Rowntree Foundation, collecting information about user-controlled alternatives to mental health services.

Kath Maines has been a member of Newcastle Mental Health Consumer Group since its inception. She is a former Chair and Secretary of the Group and has spoken at many conferences around the country on the work of the Group. Kath is currently chairing a task force for the Newcastle Mental Health Trust Board, looking at developing a comprehensive sexual harrasment policy relating to staff and patients.

Maria-Antonia Manchego-Pellanne was Acting Director of the Standing Conference of Ethnic Minority Senior Citizens until October 1992.

Majorie Mayo is a tutor at Ruskin College, Oxford, teaching on the Diploma in Social Work and Community Work courses. She has previously carried out research and published, mainly in the area of community development and community participation. She is currently Chair of the Standing Conference for Community Development.

Dave Morris is National Co-ordinator of CHOICE. Before this he founded Independent Living Alternatives and worked on consumer rights for the Office of Fair Trading. Dave is a fervent and articulate advocate for disability rights and has been recently very involved in developing theory and strategy aimed at the promotion of user-centred services.

Jenny Morris is a freelance researcher, trainer and consultant on disability issues. Her work includes training on needs-led assessment, evaluation of user-led services and development of user participation in services. Her books include *Independent Lives? Community Care and Disabled People* (Macmillan,1993) and *Pride against Prejudice: Transforming Attitudes to Disability* (Women's Press, 1991).

Terry Philpot is editor of *Community Care*. He has edited several books, including *Social Work* (1985). He is co-editor of *Practising Social Work* (to be published later this year by Routledge) and of *Values and Visions: Changing Ideas in Services for People with Learning Difficulties* (to be published next year). He is also writing a history of the National Children's Home. He is an honorary member of the council of the National Society for the Prevention of Cruelty to Children and a former member of the advisory council of the Centre for Policy on Ageing and of the social work committee of the National Children's Home.

Hardeesh K. Rai was born, brought up and educated in the Punjab, India, and came to England in 1964. She has several years experience of working with multi-ethnic communities and organisations. She is fully aware of and committed to highlighting the issues faced by minority ethnic groups when in need of welfare services. She has recently completed the Certificate of Qualification in Social Work Course at West London Institute of Higher Education. Currently, she is working as a social worker in West London with the Hounslow Social Services Department.

John Spargo has worked in a social services setting since 1971, initially in services for people with learning disabilities. He has a qualification in teaching and is particularly interested in developing consumer-centred approaches to the development and management of services in the community. John is Divisional Director for Disability Services in Hillingdon, and also has a lead role in the implementation of community care, in which he has actively promoted the involvement of service users and carers in the planning and commissioning of services.

Fenella Trevillion started her professional training in general nursing, training as a midwife. After working for some years in hospitals she joined the staff of Kaleidoscope Youth and Community Project. She then completed a sociology and politics degree at Exeter University, and following this professional social work training at Goldsmith's College. After working as a generic social worker, in 1989 she became team manager for a specialist HIV/AIDS team. Fenella is now Principal Officer for HIV Services in the London Borough of Hammersmith and Fulham.

Gareth Winn Walton was born on 2nd July 1964 in Halifax. He studied at Dewsbury and Batley Art College before leaving the farm and family he loved to move to London and embark upon his career in interior design. In 1985 he tested HIV positive at 21 years of age, in an era of lurid headlines, raging ignorance, prejudice and fear. Gareth overcame his fears and fought courageously against the prejudices of others for the right to high quality humane services for all. He died on 30th March 1993 surrounded by those he loved most.

Andrea Whittaker is Project Manager, Building Inclusive Communities which is part of the Community Care Group at the King's Fund Centre. Her work covers user participation and self-advocacy, particularly with people with learning difficulties. She has had a major involvement in the King's Fund Ordinary Life initiative and is now developing work

related to community participation. Andrea
Whittaker has been closely associated with the self-
advocacy organisation People First since it began in
1984 and was its adviser until October 1988, when
People First set up its own independent office.

Liz Wright has worked in mental health and
advocacy since 1983 when she started work in
MIND's Legal Department. Since then she has
combined work in the voluntary sector and as a self-
employed consultant, working on user-led projects
and promoting advocacy and user involvement in
mental health and other services.